making
iMovies

Use your digital camcorder and **iMac DV** to make movies for the Web

scott smith

MAKING iMOVIES
Scott Smith

Peachpit Press
1249 Eighth Street
Berkeley, CA 94710
510/524-2178
510/524-2221 (fax)

Find us on the World Wide Web at: http://www.peachpit.com

Peachpit Press is a division of Addison Wesley Longman

Copyright © 2000 Scott Smith

Editors: Marjorie Baer, Kelly Ryer, Clifford Colby
Production coordinator: Kate Reber
Copyeditors: Kelly Ryer, Lynn Kuznierz, Clifford Colby
Compositors: Lisa Brazieal, Mimi Heft
Interior design: Mimi Heft
Cover design: Mimi Heft, Zeke Zielinski
Cover illustration: Zeke Zielinski
Indexer: Rebecca R. Plunkett

ISBN 0-201-70489-7

9 8 7 6 5 4 3 2 1

Printed and bound in the United States of America

This book is dedicated to my mentor, Dan McDermott—
that rare breed of person who employs equal parts of
initiative, instruction, and inspiration to spark the creative
process in those around him. I challenged myself to emulate
this uncommon sense within the text that follows.

ACKNOWLEDGMENTS

If you've ever wondered why the acceptance speeches of Academy Award winners seem endless, it's because the more ambitious a movie project is, the more people it takes to complete it. As you will undoubtedly soon discover, moviemakers feel an acute sense of appreciation toward those who help them realize their dreams in moving pictures. To that point, there are several people who deserve recognition for their valued contributions to this book.

This project came to fruition with the assistance of Jon Bass and Carol Weiss Miller at Apple Computer Inc. and would not have developed as quickly without the foresight of Peachpit Press publisher Nancy Aldrich-Ruenzel; executive editor Marjorie Baer; my persistent editor, Kelly Ryer; and Clifford Colby, who picked up where Kelly left off. I'm also deeply indebted to Peachpit designer Mimi Heft, production coordinator Kate Reber, and compositor Lisa Brazieal, who lent their immeasurable creative and technical talents to give this book its elegant design. I am fortunate to have had counsel from both Jeff Black and Frank Grow. I also received important technical advice from the gang at Terran Interactive, particularly John Geyer, as well as Jonathan Wells, John Scalise, and John Turk, the founding editors of *RES* magazine, a bastion of the digital filmmaking community.

Beyond the task of writing, I was further challenged with the production of several short movies used to generate the raw footage used in the tutorials. Without the aid of Judy Morrissey-Pullos, Mark McDonald, and Connie Fernandez, such a feat would have been impossible. My deepest thanks go to Dan McDermott, who dedicated long hours on the set and even longer hours during the editing process.

My stable of actors were rounded up from the wide circle of talent I am extremely privileged to call family and friends. They include Kim Battisti, Mark Battisti, Steve Caroompas, Persephone Crittenden, Michelle Harvey, Ryan Martinez, Jon Schwartz, and Kathleen and Tony Morrissey. Two longtime collaborators, Zeke Zielinski and the incomparable Paddy Morrissey, were instrumental in crafting the stories and dialogue of the final movies. Even my mother, Geri Smith, graced one of the key props—the "Dear John" letter that is seen in close-up during a tutorial scene—with the elegance and beauty of her penmanship. As usual, she was also a crucial supporter throughout the writing stage of this project.

Finally, a special thanks is due to Jason Tsoi, who not only lent his acting talents to the tutorials but gave generous amounts of time and energy throughout the production of the entire book.

TABLE OF CONTENTS

No More Excuses

An Introduction

When Steve Jobs unveiled Apple's iMac DV computers last October, he spared the audience the tired phrase "revolution" and opted for a touch of understatement. "We think digital video is going to be pretty big," he stated casually. His nonchalance was perceived as supreme confidence—and for good reason. When you combine the powerful capabilities of today's consumer camcorders, personal computers, and the Internet, it's not hard to imagine a future where computer users sprinkle every email message and home page with magical cinematic moments.

What does all this mean? Well, hyperbole aside, it really does mean revolution. No significant hurdles prevent anyone interested in moviemaking from creating, editing, and distributing a film—from within the confines of their home.

Desktop video publishing is fueling the imaginations of a growing community of storytellers. Families can now send home movies to distant relatives or email a video greeting card. Local bands can easily record their own music video and display it on a home page beside their songs. Teachers, coaches, and corporate trainers can easily incorporate video into their teaching assignments, team practices, or seminars. Even Webmasters and multimedia producers can add video to an interactive project without a big investment in complex editing equipment.

Historically, moviemaking has been too complicated and expensive for the layman. Filmmakers used to expose expensive film stock through a cumbersome camera. Today, they record digital signals on reusable tapes with palm-sized camcorders. Yesterday's moviemakers spent thousands of dollars to transfer film images into computerized editing systems before manipulating the scenes; this is now done simply by capturing video footage to a hard disk. Studios used to have elaborate facilities for sound recording; now, all audio is synchronized—locked within the video signal it accompanies.

The complex, time-consuming optical processes that produced special effects for Hollywood-style films are now rendered in seconds by powerful processors built into desktop computers. Even filmmaking software was previously too technical for most artists. Too many add-in cards. Too many software drivers. Too many special settings, plug-in filters, keyboard shortcuts.

It's likely that if you're a beginning filmmaker, you can forget all the technical mumbo jumbo and take the shortest route to filmmaking. Legions of armchair directors who have long thought of making movies but have dismissed the idea because of the expense and the complexity have no more excuses. Moviemaking is no longer expensive; the combined cost of an affordable, high-quality DV camcorder and a typical multimedia PC is now less than $2,500. Moviemaking is no longer complex; all of the technologies are now included with a standard desktop computer—and the tools are remarkably simple to use. In fact, the newest models of Macintosh computers come with all of the technologies that were once the exclusive domain of video professionals.

Of course, you still need to stumble upon a great idea, audition actors, and scout locations. But frankly, the rest is simple. Armed with a few digital tools and some understanding, tomorrow's moviemakers can think of themselves as the studio producer, their PC as the studio lot, and the Internet as their screening room. Already a lot of great work from first-time directors is online.

However, the desktop video revolution will require a rethinking of nearly every aspect of traditional moviemaking. For example, the audience has changed significantly in the last several years. More people are watching movies than ever before, and many of them are watching them over the Internet. Alternative films—short subject, animation, interactive movies—have a greater acceptance among viewers than before. Online, people are proving that image resolution is not everything—story is paramount.

Even the channels of movie distribution have radically changed. The Web has subverted the traditional channels by letting filmmakers broadcast great stories directly to media-hungry viewers. Film festivals and large theater chains are struggling to keep profits high as filmmakers find their audiences through digital mediums such as DVD, cable television, and the Internet. In fact, the Internet is poised to deliver more films than any other medium, particularly in the coming broadband era.

Web movies are the latest online fashion; new sites encourage filmmakers to submit their films to add to these sites' large collections of video shorts, animated cartoons, documentaries, and comedy spoofs. In the last six months, more than 10,000 Web sites have added streaming video content to their pages. As the Internet becomes a dominant choice for exhibition of short subjects and live broadcasts, the competition among sites is heating up. However, there is clearly no clear leader in the race for superiority of Internet Cinema. Because the competition among sites is fierce, budding directors will find these sites incredibly receptive to their films. Even if it takes months to complete your next project, you can bet plenty of online forums will be eager to show your work.

Most of all, the tools have changed. The translucent, bubble-shaped iMac DV computers are essentially mini movie studios, desktop machines uniquely equipped to perform better than the giant workstations once used by filmmakers. Even full-featured editing software such as Final Cut Pro and EditDV struggle to make their high-powered, comprehensive "solutions" appealing to the consumer. It's the easy-to-use programs such as Apple's new iMovie software that have stripped the moviemaking process down to something more akin to dragging and dropping icons. These intuitive tools effectively remove the fear factor for video newbies who just want to connect their camcorders to their home computers and have everything work instantly. Apple's unique integration of key audio, video, and Internet technologies makes the iMac the only computer capable of delivering such a unified solution. In the iMac with iMovie software, video enthusiasts now have a complete production environment.

The iMovie interface was designed to make all the features of the software available in a single workshop environment. You absolutely can not get lost in the application. No cascading windows. No pull-down menus. You can see on the screen every tool you need at once. It's the most intuitive, unintimidating, and straightforward interface by far ever designed for video production. Just as Apple revolutionized the world of desktop publishing, it is now leading millions of computer users into the world of video production. There's little doubt that with the power of the iMac DV computer, the elegance of the iMovie software, and a bit of advice from this book, you will embark on a journey into the exciting world of moviemaking.

Using the Lesson Files

The instructional files provided with this book were designed to give you all of the necessary elements for completing several short movies. They include audio samples, photo scans, digital video clips, and various other files. Due to do the nature of the iMovie software, these project elements were saved in a format that best preserves their quality and allows for a seamless import into the application. To accommodate the extremely large file sizes of high-resolution DV footage, these project folders must be supplied on a DVD-ROM disc.

The individual projects are outlined below, with detailed information regarding the disk space requirements. If the disk space limitations on your iMac DV computer cannot accommodate all of the projects simultaneously, you may elect to use the projects one at a time, deleting the previous project after you have finished the lessons. In this way, you can make space available on your hard drive for the subsequent lessons.

Be careful; some of the projects and elements are featured in multiple chapters. So don't presume because the chapter has ended that the lesson files are no longer necessary. Simply look for the DVD icon in your chapter text to identify the proper files needed for each lesson.

This icon appears in chapters when referring to files that reside on the supplied DVD-ROM disc.

First Impression

Actors: Jason Tsoi, Michelle Harvey, Mark Battisti
Running Time: 1 min.

A teenager is asked to hold a skateboard for a friend and, while waiting, is approached by a girl who invites him to the upcoming dance. To impress her, he claims the skateboard as his own and must perform some tricks that are beyond his capabilities.

This lesson demonstrates the power of editing; by removing the failed attempts of an actor to execute the difficult stunts, several clips are combined to give the appearance of a successful first effort.

The Flower of Love

ACTORS: Jon Schwartz, Persephone Crittenden,
Ryan Martinez, Kim Battisti
RUNNING TIME: 2 min.

A man waits in a hotel room for a rendezvous with a woman he has never met. He reads a letter from his pen pal explaining that she will be wearing a rose on her dress. Suddenly, a woman appears. They embrace, they kiss, they look longingly at each other. When the bellhop arrives and announces the room number, they realize there has been a mistake. The woman abruptly leaves, and the man is momentarily shattered—until the real pen pal shows up.

This lesson uses music, narration, and sound effects to enhance the storytelling. Shot in black and white for a more cinematic feel, it borrows its style from the film noir look of the '30s and '40s.

General Hysteria

ACTORS: Paddy Morrissey, Steve Caroompas,
Kathleen and Tony Morrissey, Zeke Zielinski
RUNNING TIME: 2:30 min.

An army general is on the run—alone in a desert wasteland. Throughout his struggles for survival against the unrelenting forces of nature, his memory replays the events that have led him to this desperate fight for life. As the scorching sun sizzles and vultures swirl above, he suddenly wakes from his nightmare to discover that he is closer to home than first imagined.

Using the built-in transitions inside iMovie, this lesson shows the powerful ways that special effects can alter the meaning of clips. The use of cross-dissolves, fades, and wipes in the movie suggest the passage of time and form the symmetry of shots. The psychological condition of the main character is also reinforced through point-of-view shots and the overlapping narration.

Installing the Tutorial Files

To install the project files for use with the tutorial lessons:

1 Insert the Making iMovies DVD-ROM disc (provided in this book's back cover) into the slot-loading disc drive of your iMac DV computer.

2 Locate the file entitled "Making iMovies Installer" and double-click the icon.

3 After you have successfully run the installer, locate the "Project Files" folder and drag it to your hard disk. If the lesson files won't fit on your hard disk, you may wish to open the folder and transfer one lesson folder at a time.

Removing the Tutorial Files

For subsequent lessons, you can reclaim the necessary room on your hard disk by removing the previous tutorial project files and media. Simply drag the lesson folder to the Trash in the Finder and choose Empty Trash from the Special menu. This will free up valuable space for your next lesson. However, these files will not be recoverable and any changes you have saved will be lost. If you wish to retain the work you have done before removing lesson files, refer to Chapter Seven: "Saving Your Movie."

Making iMovies Installer

Restoring the Tutorial Files

At times, you may need to restore the project files from a previous lesson. To do this, insert the Making iMovies DVD-ROM disc into your iMac DV computer and locate the required files. Then, simply drag them to the appropriate location and re-launch your iMovie application. Remember, all of the project files should reside in the Media folder, alongside the original tutorial icon used to begin each lesson.

chapter one
storytelling tips

One of the biggest hurdles for would-be moviemakers is the fear that they don't have a worthwhile story to tell. It is the primary aim of this book to obliterate that misconception. Once you've overcome the outmoded notion that masterful storytelling is the domain of an elite few, you will begin to notice how stories fill the moments of your own life. In fact, we are all innate storytellers, constantly practicing our craft as we go about our daily lives.

We are all innate storytellers.

Another common phobia of the budding director is the daunting task of preparation. Many creative individuals simply throw up their hands at the idea of scriptwriting, production planning, and rehearsals. In this chapter we toss aside the antiquated Hollywood-style procedures that promote unnecessary delays—as we do throughout this book. We'll sketch just enough of the basic structure underlying effective storytelling to infuse you with the confidence you need to get started. From that point, you can begin to build a story as you create it, using the power of digital technology to free yourself from the cumbersome conventions of traditional moviemaking.

Stories Are Everywhere

Beyond the conventional storybooks, television dramas, and blockbuster movies, there are thousands of ways in which stories are presented to us every day. In fact, there is a story at the heart of every form of communication. To see it at work, consider the legions of yarnspinners and hucksters who populate your life with little tales—each delivered through greeting cards, jokes and riddles, radio commercials, music videos, instructional pamphlets, and advertising. And you—you're a storyteller too. In fact, you probably use traditional storytelling techniques dozens of times in your daily routine; when you are explaining project delays to your boss, talking your way out of a traffic ticket, or asking a sales clerk for assistance, for example. You will begin with a phrase like, "Well, this is what happened…" and conclude with a declaration like, "So next time, I won't do that again!"

There are stories happening around you all of the time. Capturing them should be your mission. Open your ears to the voices around you, and the stories will come pouring in. Listen to the experiences that people share during meals, at social gatherings, while discussing office politics, or while relating a child's sporting events. Try to absorb these stories without the filter of feasibility; don't worry whether you can tell the story with your skills and resources. Good stories shine through even the most amateur moviemaking efforts.

If you plan to showcase your movies on a Web page or share them with distant friends over email, remember that the local issues you find trivial and mundane can appear colorful and fascinating to viewers who live far away. Those tiresome anecdotes told at the annual family reunion may seem shockingly original when told to a fresh audience. Use your own expert knowledge as the basis for a story; surely there are others who share your passion for a particular hobby or interest.

Billboard Advertising Could there really be a story in a graham cracker? Here, the advertiser sets up a simple dramatic dilemma and the readers fill in the blanks: they imagine a kitchen table, a hungry child just home from school, the child eagerly bites into a favorite snack but forgets to check the fridge for the perfect complement. There in a single photograph is a story—complete with a setting, a character, and a conflict.

Event Posters This turn-of-the-century circus poster skillfully uses vignettes throughout the layout to suggest the various strength-building activities these fighters must endure to prepare for the dangerous duels they will perform before a live audience. The bustling, scattered design helps create a feeling of movement, and the final scene is highlighted in silhouette against a bright circle.

Storytelling Is About Structure

As you listen and look for inspiration in the stories of others, study the ways in which they tell those stories. Storytelling is about structure; it owes its rich and expansive heritage to familiar patterns. So, welcome a story twice told. Don't discard the opportunity to hear jokes you've already heard. Revisit the favorite songs and poems and fables of your youth to determine what has allowed them to exist so long in your memory.

Dramatic Structure

If you've ever taken a literature or writing course, it's likely that you already know everything you need to know about dramatic structure (sometimes called narrative structure). It's a basic formula: As the story begins, the main character's goal or desire is established. This goal is usually thwarted by a conflicting character or action. Tension rises as the character attempts to overcome obstacles and complications that keep the goal out of reach. Eventually, the tension will mount until it produces a climax, a breaking point, and the conflict is somehow resolved.

Much has been written of this basic formula; it appears in the structure of nearly all mythology and folklore of every civilization known to man. No matter how many times human beings see it played out, they are attracted to the tension created—momentarily or at length—before the story's conflict is resolved.

Dramatic structure takes shape in many forms. A playwright must apply this age-old formula across a three-act stage production. An author must spread the structure across several chapters. A cartoonist presents it in the form of a multi-panel gag. There are many variations and mutations, but the basic dramatic structure has remained unchanged since ancient times. Stories that fail to resolve conflict are as unsatisfying as jokes without punchlines.

No one person or company can hold claim to this structure (in fact, you should feel compelled to follow it, for it is tried and true), so you're free to emulate dramatic storytelling techniques wherever you find them. That's not to say there is no room for creativity in your movies. Stories differ mainly in the sequence of events. What makes a movie unique is the rearrangement of scenes into an interesting or original presentation of the formula. Unlike other forms of communication, movies derive added power from the juxtaposition between the picture and sound and the way in which sequences move effortlessly through time. These are excellent ways to add dimension to a story.

Most often, dramatic structure has a straightforward chronology, a step-by-step procession to the resolution of the story. Sometimes, an inventive moviemaker might choose to jumble the sequence of events to breathe life into the old formula. For instance, flashbacks, premonitions, and time travel are all common devices used to shake up the chronological order of a movie's story. Other moviemakers may embrace a well-worn structure that sets up the audience for an expected ending and suddenly twist events in humorous or surprising ways.

How-To Articles Often, scientific and engineering magazines such as *Popular Mechanics* will spice up an article with a simple dramatic structure. By placing photographs at both ends of this step-by-step procedure for fixing a flat tire, the magazine tells a story. The man has a flat, follows a course of actions, and is back on the road. Just imagine the article without the two photographs, and you'll see how a story structure immediately adds interest to an otherwise dry subject.

Comic Strips The funny pages contain excellent examples of story structure at work in our everday lives. We read comics in the same way we watch movies—we follow a linear story through a series of dramatic progressions. In this gag from the popular "Nancy" comic strip, the conflict is established immediately. Sluggo is in a boxing match. Several reaction shots of Nancy lead us directly to the dramatic quandary: Will Sluggo outlast this larger and more aggressive foe? Cartoonist Ernie Bushmiller helps the story visually by making both Nancy and the opponent more agitated as the strip progresses. He also breaks several panels into smaller sizes to create a sense of urgency. Notice how the second series of quick punches are drawn smaller still, to suggest even faster flurries of action. Of course, the emotional resolution of the story comes when we realize that Sluggo is not concerned at all.

TITLE	REACTION SHOT	QUICK ACTION	REACTION	QUICK ACTION	FINAL RESOLUTION
ESTABLISHING ACTION		QUICK ACTION		QUICK ACTION	

Structure at Work A breakdown of this comic strip reveals the storytelling structure used by the cartoonist to heighten the dramatic tension. Studying these simple story forms in the daily newspaper can help you create your own movies.

Getting Your Story Started

If you've already got videotapes lying around the house, each filled with precious footage, you are ready to begin making movies without any further planning. Buried in those hours of recorded events may be enough material to create a perfect story. Perhaps all you need is some attention to structure.

Shoot First, Structure Later

The beauty of iMovie is that you can pick up your camcorder and start recording ideas without a comprehensive plan for every scene, every line of dialogue, and every actor's motion. Just shoot wildly and make it up as you go. If you don't like the footage, you can always erase the tapes and reshoot. For home moviemakers, there's no risk or cost associated with doing this.

Reshoots are virtually unheard of in Hollywood studios. Occasionally, when a movie fails to receive great audience approval at previews and screenings, a gifted director or a savvy producer might deem it necessary to replace or remove footage from a scene—even if this means assembling the actors and tradesmen for a reshoot. Fortunately, DV technology makes reshoots simple and affordable.

You may want to shoot a few scenes, structure them in iMovie, reshoot the ones you don't like, replace them with new footage, and restructure them until you are satisfied with the results. You can shoot, structure, reshoot, and restructure to your heart's content. Master joketellers do this endlessly, always perfecting their setup and delivery, crafting the perfect opening, honing the timing of the punchline, and whittling the joke down to its bare essentials. Just as brevity is the soul of wit, economy is the key to effective storytelling. Only by restructuring your story can you discover more efficient ways of getting your point across.

Circumvent the Script

The most profound change that the digital video revolution has brought to the moviemaking process is the plausibility of making movies without a script. And what a welcome change it is. Frankly, screenwriting can be daunting for the budding moviemaker, and too many good visual artists have stifled their careers believing they couldn't make this initial step. There have been some wonderful filmmakers who were also wonderful writers, and there have also been some great directors who never relied on a script when filming. Precedents aside, the quickest way to get your story started is to forget about a script.

Historically, the reliance on scripts came about in the silent era of cinema, when Hollywood studios suddenly found the demand for their pictures increasing and needed to produce several films simultaneously. Used largely for continuity, the script became an essential communication tool between the lone producer or director and the hundreds of actors and tradesmen struggling to remember all of the details. Without a script, any delay or miscue on the set could result in escalating costs. Expensive film stock could be wasted or damaged. Union craftsmen might demand overtime pay. Actors on loan from other studios might have to return to other productions. Scripts helped filmmakers avoid delays, saving the studios money.

These conditions no longer apply. Yet today, independent filmmakers follow the traditions of the past almost blindly, spending a great deal of time on scripts and screenplays. Ironically, they often find that much of their script is tossed out when the constraints of shooting on location force them to make last-minute compromises.

Scripts are not altogether useless; they can be helpful in planning long projects, or those which require careful stunts or special effects. Scripts are a great way for writers to articulate a vision to the person who will ultimately direct the movie. They are ideal for big corporations that must pass an idea around its bureaucratic decision mill. But scripts are hardly a necessity for a one-person production. If you are the only writer/producer/director/soundman/technician/editor who will be working on your movie, you are the only one who can determine if a script is necessary.

Storyboards

While scripts are superfluous, storyboards are an ideal way to develop your ideas. A storyboard is a series of individual pictures which, once combined (usually pinned to a wall or bulletin board) into a structured organization, help a moviemaker conceptualize the final movie. Often, visual artists will outline every action of a scene in remarkable detail. Other filmmakers use storyboards strictly for story pacing, choosing to keep the specific actions undefined until shooting begins. Storyboards are an effective way to analyze your story's structure, focusing on themes rather than camera placement and dialogue. They are used extensively by animation studios, which must make sure the story is solid before proceeding with the arduous job of drawing the frames.

Although sometimes referred to as "picture scripts," storyboards don't need to be composed entirely of images. Most storyboards combine dialogue cards with inspirational sketches to achieve a balance. It is quite common to see blank pieces of paper, representing a break between scenes or suggesting a transition effect. Some storyboards use photographs as placeholder images, and many work effectively with nothing but words.

Better still, you don't need to be an artist to create storyboards. You can use clippings from magazines, comic book illustrations, Polaroid photographs, and handwritten index cards. You can enlarge or reduce images on a photocopier and place each on a single sheet so you can conveniently move them around when you are assembling your story. These days, you don't even need to pin anything on a bulletin board. With your home computer, you might wish to scan images or download them from Web pages and incorporate them into your storyboards.

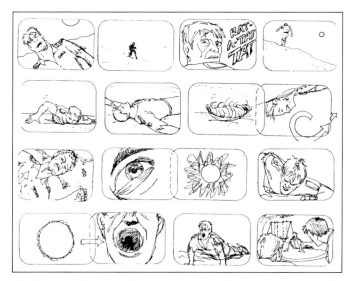

Vital Scenes of Action The storyboards used to create the tutorial movies were kept to a single page. These loose drawings provide a good sense of the vital action required to communicate the story's main points without too much detail regarding camera placement, actor movement, or specific dialogue.

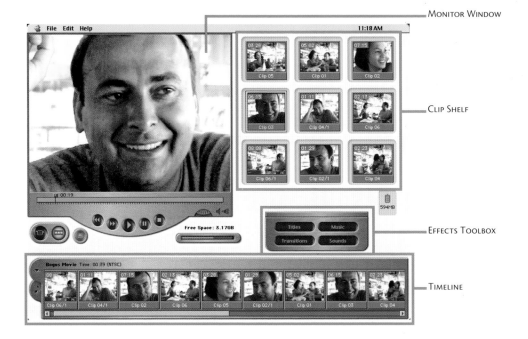

MONITOR WINDOW

CLIP SHELF

EFFECTS TOOLBOX

TIMELINE

Using iMovie to Structure Stories

The iMovie interface is ideal for organizing your footage in intuitive ways. You can easily import still images, Web graphics, or scanned drawings to supplement any missing footage while you develop the structure for your stories.

The Clip Shelf

Much like a storyboard mounted on a wall, the Clip Shelf in iMovie provides an ideal workspace for arranging your picture elements into a story structure. You can drag video clips and imported images from place to place in the Clip Shelf until you find an order that works best for telling your story.

Imagine you have previously recorded a grandparent reading a book to a child. You captured the footage in iMovie and placed it in the Clip Shelf, but you may need additional footage to complete your story. You can scan pictures from the book, import them into iMovie, and spread them throughout the footage to help illustrate the story. Or maybe you'd like to show old family photographs as the grandparent reads. This kind of experimentation is fast and flexible when you use the iMovie software.

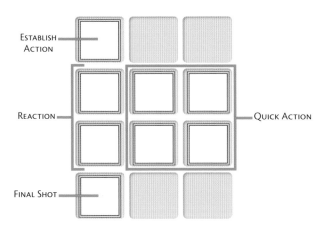

ESTABLISH ACTION

REACTION

QUICK ACTION

FINAL SHOT

Structuring Clips By dragging video clips and imported images around the empty spaces and rows of iMovie's Clip Shelf, you can discover which sequence works best for telling your story.

LESSON: BUILDING STORYBOARDS IN iMOVIE

To demonstrate ways in which iMovie can help you structure your stories and explore ideas for dialogue, narration, and sound effects, the Building Storyboards project uses images scanned directly from an actual storyboard. A sample of the finished movie, Flower.mov, can be found in the QuickTime Gallery folder on the DVD-ROM disc.

To begin this lesson, launch the iMovie application and open the project called Storyboard Lesson.

This sample storyboard, developed for one of the tutorial movies used in this book, was created to fit on a single sheet of paper. When creating storyboards, highlight the main scenes or shots and explain the actions within the scenes in text below each illustration.

Sample Storyboard Developed for one of the tutorial movies used in this book, these illustrations were created to highlight the main shots and explain the actions within the scenes. Try to keep your storyboards short, even to a single sheet of paper.

◀ **1** Choose Open Project from the File Menu.

2 Locate the Building Storyboards folder and select the StoryBoard Lesson project.

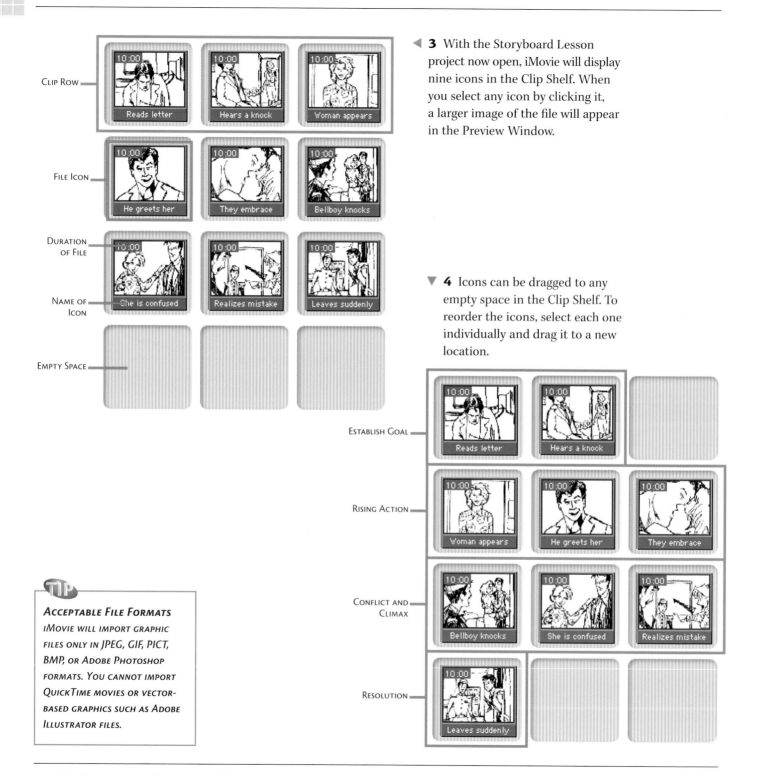

CLIP ROW

FILE ICON

DURATION OF FILE

NAME OF ICON

EMPTY SPACE

Reads letter | Hears a knock | Woman appears
He greets her | They embrace | Bellboy knocks
She is confused | Realizes mistake | Leaves suddenly

3 With the Storyboard Lesson project now open, iMovie will display nine icons in the Clip Shelf. When you select any icon by clicking it, a larger image of the file will appear in the Preview Window.

4 Icons can be dragged to any empty space in the Clip Shelf. To reorder the icons, select each one individually and drag it to a new location.

ESTABLISH GOAL — Reads letter | Hears a knock

RISING ACTION — Woman appears | He greets her | They embrace

CONFLICT AND CLIMAX — Bellboy knocks | She is confused | Realizes mistake

RESOLUTION — Leaves suddenly

ACCEPTABLE FILE FORMATS
iMOVIE WILL IMPORT GRAPHIC FILES ONLY IN JPEG, GIF, PICT, BMP, OR ADOBE PHOTOSHOP FORMATS. YOU CANNOT IMPORT QUICKTIME MOVIES OR VECTOR-BASED GRAPHICS SUCH AS ADOBE ILLUSTRATOR FILES.

HIGHLIGHT INDICATES SELECTION

◄ **5** To duplicate a clip, drag your cursor over the icon and click once to select it. A yellow highlight will appear around the edges of your clip. The image will also appear in the larger Preview Window.

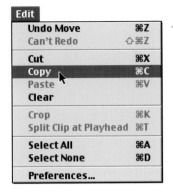

◄ **6** Choose Copy from the Edit menu. (The keyboard shortcut for this command is Command–C.)

◄ **7** Next, choose Paste from the Edit menu. (The keyboard shortcut for this command is Command–V.)

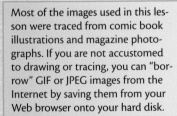  

◄ **8** By placing your cursor over the name of an icon and clicking, you will highlight the text below it. Once highlighted, the text can be edited by simply typing a new name.

CREATING IMAGES FOR IMPORT INTO iMOVIE

Most of the images used in this lesson were traced from comic book illustrations and magazine photographs. If you are not accustomed to drawing or tracing, you can "borrow" GIF or JPEG images from the Internet by saving them from your Web browser onto your hard disk.

(Of course, many of the images on the Web are copyrighted, so you'll want to use them only as placeholders.)

When you are scanning or creating storyboard illustrations in an image-manipulation program such as Adobe Photoshop, you'll want to use

an image size of 640 × 480, for they will appear in the iMovie Preview Window and Clip Shelf as full images and icons. When you import photos or illustrations that are smaller than that size, they'll appear with a black border surrounding their edges.

LESSON: IMPORTING PICT AND JPEG IMAGES

You can add files to the Clip Shelf by importing graphic files in a number of popular file formats. This is an excellent way to enhance your storyboards as you experiment with story structure.

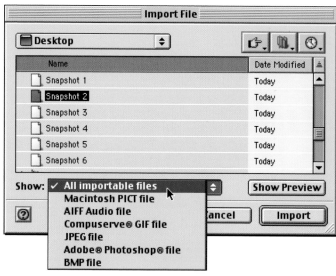

◀ **1** With the Storyboard Lesson still open, choose Import File from the File menu.

▲ **2** A dialog box will appear, prompting you to select the file you wish to import. Select the file called Drawing 10.jpg from the Building Storyboards folder.

▶ **3** Drag the icon to the appropriate position on the Clip Shelf and change its name to reflect the story.

▲ **4** You might want to use the text beneath the icons to suggest a line of dialogue in your storyboards. Keep your text short; clip icons can display names of only 10 to 26 characters in length.

5 To keep your revisions, choose Save from the File menu.

PRINTING THE CLIP SHELF

YOU MAY WANT TO PRINT THE CLIP SHELF AREA OF THE MONITOR SCREEN TO USE AS A REFERENCE DURING SHOOTING. YOU CAN DO THIS BY TYPING COMMAND-SHIFT-4 ON YOUR KEYBOARD. A CROSSHAIR CURSOR WILL APPEAR. DRAG THE CROSSHAIR TO DEFINE WHICH PART OF THE SCREEN YOU WANT TO CAPTURE AND LET GO. A "PICTURE" FILE WILL BE SAVED TO YOUR HARD DRIVE. LOCATE IT AND PRINT IT USING THE SIMPLETEXT APPLICATION, WHICH COMES PRE-INSTALLED ON YOUR IMAC COMPUTER.

Showing and Telling

Movies have virtually all the advantages of other mediums. Like a great painting or stage show, they can dazzle the eyes. Like a radio program or a symphony, they can spark the imagination with sound. Best of all, movies can do all of these things at once. Where visuals add mood, narration can add tone. Mood and tone together are a potent combination, so it's important to think about both sound and pictures when developing a story.

In fact, the best cinematic moments are those that skillfully combine beautiful imagery with a perfect auditory complement. For example, "trigger" actions in movies—the shot of a gun, a woman's scream—are best punctuated with a strikingly clear picture accompanied by a startling sound effect.

There are several effective ways to mix visual action and narration to enhance your stories. Typically, it is better to "show" primary action visually and secondary story points with sound. Dialogue is best used to illustrate parts of the story that would disrupt the narrative if they were shown visually. For example, if two men are leaving for a party, and they expect to meet a woman there, it is more effective to explain in dialogue that the woman is on the way than to cut to footage showing the woman preparing for the event, hailing a cab, stuck in traffic, and so on. Overall, sound and visual information should be unified by a driving action—the two men heading to the event—which keeps the story progressing through time.

Movies are more than just simultaneous sound and pictures. What makes them unique is their ability to depict the events of characters as they march toward a goal. This should be your guiding principle in storytelling.

chapter two

shooting techniques

Generally, moviemakers hate to receive advice on shooting. This is understandable, considering that the choices made in developing shots have been the hallmark of a moviemaker's style for more than 100 years now. Therefore, most of the advice dispensed in this chapter is offered humbly, as suggestions to help you combat the unique challenges of presenting your movie over the Internet. Making movies for the Internet is not altogether different from making films for a theater, but several distinctions will call for special attention during shooting. Shooting alone as a single cameraman, or armed with a small band of loyal revolutionaries, you have advantages that no studio can match. In fact, you've got the upper hand. As the inconspicious boss of your own home studio Tinseltown will never see you coming. You're a guerrilla moviemaker with more independence and spirit than Hollywood could hope to muster. While they spend gazillions on the next period drama, costume spectacle, and deep-sea action sequel, you can use your keen insight, coupled with a bit of Web-based wisdom, to build your own empire online.

You have advantages no studio can match.

Neighborhood Moviemaking

If desktop video technology spawns a revolution on the Web, it will likely be in the proliferation of "neighborhood" movies—the small, powerful stories that have been cloistered in their communities mainly because they were never deemed worthy of silver screen projection. Neighborhood moviemakers celebrate the uniqueness of their hometown, the people around them, the cultural events and industries that define their surroundings; they can hail from hippie communes, factory towns, or coastal resorts. They let others specialize in unreal places, bizarre science fictions, imaginary creatures, and supernatural powers. They turn their cameras on their own village, and by posting the results on the Web, they can share the universal hopes and fears of their neighbors with viewers around the world.

Shoot It Locally, Show It Globally

The fabric of your moviemaking style can be further textured by using the landmarks of your local surroundings as the backdrop for your stories. Why travel great distances to shoot your video, when most Web audiences will find your own neighborhood as foreign to them as a remote planet?

It may take some training to scout locations nearby. You may have become so acclimated to your own streets, parks, and buildings that you pass them unaware of the awe they could inspire in unfamiliar eyes. As you consider local monuments, statues of famous citizens, or architectural marvels, attempt to look at these things from a new angle.

Use Actors You Already Know

Discovering talent in the people you interact with is a joy of moviemaking. The only way to know if there is a dormant actor among your friends or family members is to stick a camcorder into their faces and ask for a reading. You'll be amazed. Characters will reveal themselves in strange ways. And don't be surprised if the class clown or family prankster doesn't turn up gold. Hamming seldom produces a good performance in close-up. The most subtle and reserved expressions translate best to the moving image. So look around for the wallflower.

Your new role as casting director will demand some sharp observation. Keep your eyes on people at every moment; they are acting all the time—in conversation, in presentations, even in moments of solitude. It's likely that your acting troupe is closer than you think.

If mining the neighborhood doesn't turn up a few actors, don't give up! Check local theater productions or comedy clubs. In many cases, local musicians, athletes, and public leaders are a good bet; they are comfortable with performing. These local faces can lend local color to your movies.

Spare Every Expense

To get your shoot off the ground, do everything possible to reduce the expense and complexity of your scenes. Simplify your stunts, don't rely on special effects, and use the props you have readily available to you. If you need to purchase items for costumes or props, scour neighborhood garage sales and secondhand stores for bargains on the materials you need. These resources can keep your costs low while giving your sets and actors some interest. Asking actors to create their own costumes is a great way to get them excited about their characters.

Cast Your Friends Actor Paddy Morrissey, the star of the *General Hysteria* tutorial movie, is an accomplished stand-up comedian with years of stage and television experience. Fortunately, he also happens to be the author's co-worker—a stroke a luck for the casting department!

Shooting for the Web

When making movies for the Internet, you should begin with the end in mind—think about exactly how this movie will be seen. If you are new to moviemaking, this consideration will form the foundation for your shot selections. If you are an experienced filmmaker, you will be dealing with a completely new set of rules that may contradict the lessons you've learned. You must break old habits and preconceived notions to understand the dynamics of this new medium.

Watching Net cinema is a radically different experience than seeing a movie in a theater. The width of the screen—the monitor window of most multimedia players—is three inches wide, not thirty feet long. The typical Web surfer huddles only 15 inches away from the image, not 150 feet away in a comfortable reclining chair. Because Internet users browse the Web on a variety of different computers, there is no way of telling which monitor resolution and speakers they will be using. However, you can bet that they're a far cry from the 70mm wide-screen projection with DTS surround sound systems commonly found in today's moviehouses.

The factors that determine how your movie will appear over the Web are governed by the video compression software used to squeeze your raw DV signal into a QuickTime file. The compression software that is built into iMovie can intelligently analyze each frame of your footage to reduce the overall file size while retaining the integrity of the final images. However, the quality of Web-compressed video depends on the movement and luminance of the original source material. The old adage "garbage in, garbage out" is acutely relevant to DV footage. For this reason, it may be useful to consider several shooting methods that can dramatically improve the Web movie experience.

Some Shots Are Not Web-Friendly

Until advances in broadband technology make slower Internet access speeds a thing of the past, there are real-world issues to consider if your audience is viewing your movies over a 56K modem, DSL, cable modem, or even high-speed T1 connections. As movies are downloaded or streamed over the Web, their playback performance is affected by the movie's file size and compression ratio.

That's a lot of mumbo jumbo, but it basically boils down to this: Reduce the amount of fast and extended motion in your movie, and it will appear at an improved rate. That may sound oxymoronic (if you take out the fast stuff, your movie will speed up), but it's true. High-speed action sequences mean sluggish playback.

Luminance, or the lack of it, also plays an important role. Dark scenes are difficult to compress, so you should avoid videotaping in low-light conditions. Even though you think a situation may be lit well enough to look good on a television set, the scene may not compress well enough to display accurately over the Web.

HOW VIDEO COMPRESSION WORKS

Video compression is the digital equivalent of making concentrated orange juice. The iMovie software squeezes the image data of your finished digital movie to 1/8000 of its original signal quality, producing high-quality clips that are optimized for the Web. Naturally, compressing video to this extreme means chucking away much of the image clarity. But there are ways to make sure your footage leaves a good impression over the Web. To start, it helps to keep your action smooth. Jerky movements and flash-cutting will prevent the compression software from working its magic. The mathematical algorithms used in compression tools look for similar patterns across the pixels of many frames. So when you rapidly change images in editing, you rob yourself of compression savings. Isolated areas of movement are better, static close-ups are best. You should also avoid heavy patterns in costumes or sets, as they also compress poorly. Armed with a few shooting tips, and any of today's powerful compression tools, anyone can shoot video that is well suited for streaming over the Web.

Think About Contrast

Concentrate on creating compositions with high contrast between light and dark but with consistent tones of colors in medium hues. On the Web, contrast is more important than color. More to the point, colors will be displayed inconsistently on different monitors, so it is best not to rely on color accuracy as a means of identifying characters or objects that are critical to your story.

As a rule, keep details in the background to a minimum. While shooting your actors in close-up, try to adjust the focus to diffuse any distracting objects or patterns in the background. Make sure you are shooting against an unchanging background.

A large brick pattern on a wall is all right; the pattern is stationary and the color tone is consistent. A scene that has bushes and trees blowing in the wind is undesirable, because they create shifting patterns and variations in color tone that will prevent the compression software from reducing the final file size of your movie.

Use Contrast Contrast can help isolate important actions or draw attention to objects, such as the letter the man is reading in this scene. The sharp contrast of his white shirt against the dark suit will help the compression software.

Beware of Backgrounds The actor appears in a tight, intricate patchwork created by the small bricks, making it more difficult for compression software to consistently track over many frames. The result will be a shifting pattern that jitters during playback.

Closing In A composition that closes in on the actor can salvage the strong contrast and medium tones but creates a large, distinct pattern of bricks that is better suited for compression.

Use Close-ups in Your Compositions

In the history of cinema, the close-up has done more to craft the careers of legendary screen idols than the directors who choreograph them. Close-up shots draw the audience into the story, creating a sense of intimacy with the characters. To convey complex emotional reactions, and in some cases the sheer beauty of the human face, the camera must shorten the distance between the audience and the actors by enlarging images until they fill the screen.

Medium and close-up shots also tend to produce the best color and image sharpness, which will significantly improve the quality of your movie after compression. However, you should avoid the practice of zooming in for close-up shots, as this will require the computer to compress the entire frame instead of just the subtle changes in facial features. Zooming in on a face will alter every aspect, every pixel of the picture frame—and it forces the computer to adjust for every shift in color, pattern, and movement, ultimately reducing the effectiveness of the compression software. This can result in slow and jerky video playback when streamed over the Internet.

Getting Closer Big faces in the frame exclude undesirable elements and gain intimacy. Close-ups draw the audience into the emotional state through a greater range of subtlety and nuance, which helps create a rapport with the viewer.

Examining Your Shots This medium shot of two actors seems well conceived on the surface; however, the presence of people in the background, the reflective surface of the trash can, and the rustling branches of the tree will create enough activity in the frame to inhibit compression.

Rearranging Compositions Now, the dark hair of the boy is nicely contrasted by the sky, and the blonde hair of the girl is nested into the dark background of the tree. The branches, although still not ideal, are now larger and more defined.

Silhouette Vital Scenes of Action

Close-ups are great, but successful movies vary their visuals by providing a hearty mix of close, medium, and long shots. Many actions work well in all shots. For example, a handshake can be videotaped in close-up by isolating just the two hands as they meet; a medium shot would include the actors from the waist up; and a long shot would expose their entire forms as they approach each other.

Long shots are identified as images that include the full figure of the actor, from head to toe. Long shot compositions struggle to communicate the subtleties of the face, so they are typically used to stage broader actions, like fight scenes and other stunts. When composing shots that include these broad actions, particularly those that may be vital to the understanding of the plot, it's important to consider the position of the actors and their movements.

The use of silhouetting in your compositions can help immeasurably, especially when actions are displayed inside the small window of a computer monitor. Silhouetted actions are those so clearly defined that they would be distinguishable even if projected in two monochromatic colors (or in pitch black against stark white).

Staging Actions Clearly The silhouetted shot is vital to actions in this scene. By staging the actor in profile, the movement of his arms, the lifting of the canteen, and the act of drinking, are absolutely clear to viewers—even when viewed through a 3-inch browser window.

Moving Within a Single Setup Avoid camera zooms, where every pixel in the frame changes slightly as you close in. Instead, set up your actors to enter, pause midway into the room, and move again until they draw near the camera. As with a zoom, there is fluid movement, but most of the elements in the frame will not change position. These critical actions, all performed during the actor's entrance, give the impression of three separate compositions.

Avoid Bad Staging Many vital actions cannot be deciphered when displayed on the Web. Here, the action of drinking from a canteen is obscured by the positioning of the actor in front view.

Turn to Profile By turning the actor in profile, the action becomes easier to identify for your audience. When reduced to the size of a credit card, this movement will remain clear.

Add Dramatic Flair It's important to exaggerate movements for purposes of clarity. This back-bending drink instantly suggests a thirstier character than the one who casually sips.

Issues with Camera Movement

Sudden horizontal movement, like fast panning, is a nightmare for video compression software (mysteriously, vertical panning doesn't affect compression to the same degree, but it's a less popular shooting device). If you must include a fast sweep of camera movement, try to restrict the panning to a short burst—then settle the frame on its destination and hold for a few seconds. This generally produces better Web video.

Zooming is also troublesome. Instead of using your camcorder's zoom feature during your videotaping, try to stage scenes so you can take a static shot, pause the recording, zoom in for a close-up, and resume the recording. Another solution is to have the actors move within the scene to create several compositions within a single setup. This stabilizes many of the elements in the frame but gives the scene a variety of interesting compositions without additional camerawork.

Dressing up for DV

As with all movie shoots, it's important to pay attention to small problems that costumes can cause for the camera. Basically, you want to reduce any chance that the wardrobe might interfere with the way your camcorder records light and sound. Shiny jewelry, slick hair, metallic fabrics, and patent leather can often reflect light into the lens. Certain hats and hairstyles may cast awkward shadows over the faces of the actors. Some costumes may clank or rustle during movement, creating strange noises that make a crucial line of dialogue inaudible. Most important, pay close attention to the colors and patterns of the clothing your actors choose to wear.

SHUTTER SPEED SETTINGS
CHECK YOUR CAMCORDER FOR ADJUSTMENTS THAT WILL SLOW THE SHUTTER SPEED, A DIGITAL EFFECT THAT CAN REDUCE HIGH-SPEED CAMERA MOTION. IF YOU ARE COMPELLED TO USE FAST PANNING DURING YOUR SHOOTS, THIS FEATURE CAN IMPROVE THE RESULTS OF YOUR VIDEO.

Choosing Costumes The costumes worn in "The Flower of Love" tutorial were chosen to look best in black and white. A dark suit was rejected for one with medium gray tones and no distinct weave in the fabric. The woman's blouse includes large roses in sharp contrast to the black cloth.

Using Camera Effects Further attention was paid to how costumes would complement the actors when shooting in black and white. Using the digital picture effects built into the DV camcorder, the movie was recorded in black and white directly to a Mini-DV tape and imported into iMovie.

Here are a few pointers on selecting the right costumes:

- **Avoid fabrics that wrinkle easily.** This is important for two reasons. First, the constant pattern of shifting wrinkles will make it harder for the software to compress your movie to a compact file size. Second, wrinkles are tell-tale signs; if you need to place a clip of the actor's last take near the beginning of a scene, it may look awkward that the shirt is wrinkled when he enters the room but becomes smoother as the scene progresses.

- **Avoid tightly woven patterns in your fabrics** (such as checkers and stripes) that may cause a jittering effect in the video signal when the character is moving. Patterns with contrasting colors will often appear to vibrate, giving off the impression that the costume is glowing.

- **Avoid colors that are extremely light or extremely dark.** There are several good reasons for this. Characters wearing white—or even off-white—shirts may reflect too much light around their own face and the faces of actors nearby. In bright conditions, elements of white clothing sometimes get overexposed, and details like pockets, buttons, and collars become indistinguishable from the shirt. Details in dark blue and near-black clothing are equally difficult to differentiate even with professional camera lighting. Watch out for circumstances that put actors wearing dark colors against a dark background—in many cases, their heads will appear to be floating in a sea of darkness. A good rule of thumb is to stick to varying colors of clothing in medium tones and look for optimal light in all situations.

Using Your DV Camcorder

Stand Still, Shut Up, and Focus

Nothing is more exasperating than watching a piece of potentially powerful footage that has been undermined by the cameraman's jerky shooting techniques. Time and again, editors have yanked hair from their heads in response to such footage, practically screaming, "Stand still, shut up, and focus." Of course, the term "focus" here is used as a technical point, referring to maintaining a sharp picture at all times. But it certainly implies the other meaning of the word as well—stay alert as you are recording video.

Stand Still

Patience is a worthwhile trait to cultivate if you plan to make movies; steady, smooth camera movement delivers the best results. Fortunately, most digital camcorders have some kind of image stabilization built in. And most of them are lightweight, so holding the camera in a stationary position should not produce too much strain.

Although it's not essential for shooting, a sturdy tripod will help remove the camera operator's natural body movement. If you do not own a tripod and don't want to spend money on one, you can find other ways of stabilizing the camera during shooting. When standing up, place the elbow of your support arm firmly against your body, using the other hand on the camera body for guidance.

Better yet, put the camera down on a solid surface during shooting. Find creative ways to use everyday objects for interesting camera locations. The top of a bookshelf, a tabletop, or a sturdy crate can be used to support the weight of the camera at different angles. Even outdoors, you can discover some wonderful camera supports. At the park, try using a seesaw for a tilt shot that gives the look of a professional crane in motion.

There's no need to shy away from hand-held shots; they provide a wonderful vitality to certain scenes. Simply be aware of the degree to which your picture is jittering. Most of today's consumer-level digital camcorders have excellent stabilization technology built into their circuitry. You may also want to consult the owner's manual for additional features that help steady the images as you record them. Remarkably, what can't be straightened out in the camera can often be fixed during compression. While some software compression utilities have difficulty dealing with hand-held camera work, many video codecs (including those built into iMovie's Export feature) can intelligently detect and compensate for slight motion in your footage.

Don't become overly concerned with products like Steadicam and gyro-based gizmos for smoothing out your motion. In fact, here's a little secret: These gadgets seldom work for camera operators who aren't trained in their use. The trick is really in the way you walk and swivel

CAMERAS USED FOR THE TUTORIAL MOVIES

The tutorial movies provided for the lessons were all shot on low-cost, consumer-grade digital camcorders. We used the Sony TRV7 for most of the shooting, although the lightweight Sony DVCR-PC1 was used interchangeably without a noticeable difference in picture quality. Both cameras feature adjustable color viewfinders, which alleviate the need to press the eyepiece against the face and greatly reduce the jitters! These cameras also contain controls for white balance, exposure settings, and picture effects (like sepia tone or black and white), which were used extensively. Manual focus is another valuable feature. Although both cameras were made by Sony, many excellent FireWire camcorders are available from Canon, JVC, and others. Check the "Related Links" appendix for a list of their Web sites.

your body as you hold the camera unit. Steadicam operators learn to glide with their footsteps from the heel to the balls of their feet as they walk, keeping their knees in a bent position and shifting their body weight slightly in anticipation of a corner turn or change of direction. Watching a cameraman perform with a Steadicam is much like seeing a duck waddle or a speed walker walk. One foot rolls gently in front of the other, and the camera seems to float along the same plane. With practice, you should be able to take great hand-held footage using these same techniques—without the expense of "professional" equipment.

Shut Up

There's not a nice way to say this: Keep quiet, pipe down, zip it. The reason is quite simple—DV audio is automatically synchronized with video the instant it is recorded. Having the audio perfectly synced to the moving images is a marvelous advancement for moviemakers, for it removes the endless complexities that filmmakers encounter when recording sound independently and mixing it in postproduction.

Synchronized audio presents a good news/bad news quandary. The good news is that the quality of the built-in microphones and recording levels of today's DV camcorders is entirely adequate for most shoots. The bad news is that the equipment is so sensitive that it can pick up the slightest sounds on set: the breathing of the camera operator, birds flying overhead, traffic and crowd noises. Most often, these sounds help create a sense of reality. When they are unwanted, however, you might need to use external microphones or get your sound effects in other ways.

Make sure you fully understand the way your DV camcorder records audio. Locate the built-in microphone on the camera and shield it from any disruptive noises that may prevent viewers from hearing the actors' dialogue. Computer hard drives, refrigerators, car engines, and windy weather can create low-frequency noises that are often ignored by the human ear on the set but are distinct enough to be heard on the DV tape when recorded. These sounds can interfere with your ability to make movies that have a cohesive soundtrack.

DV audio is extremely high quality, so it is likely to be your best source. You can enlist the help of remote microphones or professional sound equipment if you feel compelled to, but silence remains the most effective weapon against unwanted noise.

Focus

Focus is the key to consistently matching your shots in editing. Imagine watching an intense dialogue exchange between two actors in close-up shots, and suddenly a piece of footage is blurry and soft. The distraction is too great to ignore, and most viewers will resent the disruption. Thankfully, this scenario is becoming rare in the digital age.

Magically, today's digital cameras have an innate sense for keeping things sharp. Their automatic focus features can make adjustments that are too subtle for the human eye. Most attempts to override this sophisticated technology with manual control only prevents the camera from achieving maximum clarity. In matters of focus, let the camera do its job.

However, in bustling environments, or even when actors are simply moving from the foreground to the background of the frame, your camera's auto-focus may take a few seconds to select the correct lens position. The effect is a muddled mess of images that can ruin a great take. In this case, you can deactivate the auto-focus features and choose a manual setting with a longer focal depth to approximate the full range of movement.

AVOID 16:9 FORMAT
SOME MOVIEMAKERS ARE ATTRACTED TO A FEATURE OF MANY DIGITAL CAMCORDERS THAT RECORDS IMAGES IN A HOLLYWOOD–STYLE LETTERBOXED FORMAT— A RATIO REFFERED TO AS 16:9. THIS FORMAT ADDS BLACK BANDS ACROSS THE TOP AND BOTTOM OF THE VIDEO FOOTAGE. THE HORIZONTAL LOOK IS APPEALING; HOWEVER, IMOVIE DOES NOT WORK WITH CLIPS WITH A 16:9 ASPECT RATIO. THEREFORE, THIS FEATURE SHOULD NOT BE USED WHEN SHOOTING.

Know Your Camera

A good deal of your creative decisions can come from a thorough understanding of your camera. Although most consumers never read the manuals that accompany their purchases, today's electronics manufacturers go to substantial lengths to inform you about the creative and technical possibilities of your digital equipment. Don't underestimate this valuable resource; there is a wealth of advice on the care and operation of your camcorder that will help in troubleshooting problems. Invest the short time it takes to browse through these materials, for your knowledge will be reflected in the quality of your finished movies.

Looking Like a Pro

The main tools at a moviemaker's disposal are light, sound, and space. Much of cinema's greatness as an art form has been accredited to the power of images that are enhanced by these elements, mainly in concert with another.

Tips on Lighting

Lighting is a moviemaker's most important tool. Professional cinematographers use lights as a painter uses a palette of colors. Perhaps that's why directors often refer to the craft of cinematography as "painting with light." In fact, many directors of photography study the works of Dutch and Italian painters, desperately attempting to re-create on film the masterly representations of lighting on canvas.

Adjusting Exposure Most of today's consumer-level DV camcorders do a great job of adjusting to changes in natural light. However, you may wish to adjust the camera's exposure controls to enhance the intensity of some shots.

Outdoor Lighting Natural sunlight is an excellent light source for many situations. Overcast skies and early morning sunrises provide ideal conditions. This shot was recorded at sunset to give a golden hue to the movie's final scene.

Picture Effects Digital camcorders offer adjustable settings for exposure and white balance. These controls can make your footage look bright and overexposed or produce shifts in the color hue that cast a blue or yellow tone across the entire frame.

With that said, there is really nothing mystical about setting up indoor lighting for the camera. Typically, most interior scenes use a three-light setup, where a main light source provides the brightest illumination on the subject, and two smaller light sources act as highlights for the back and sides of the same object. These smaller lights often serve to distance the subject from its background and diffuse the shadows created by the main light source. There's nothing to it—almost 80% of all shots are captured using these three simple light sources.

Never shoot video in low-light conditions with the intention of making it brighter (enhancing its luminance) in a computer program; this is just bad policy. Dark footage produces troublesome noise in the details of shadowed areas. This noise may not seem problematic at first, but the fluttering artifacts that it produces when compressed can be very distracting to the viewer.

Recording Ambient Noises for Sound Effects

Yelling "Quiet on the set!" is a smart way to get a clear audio recording while shooting dialogue. But you may also need to record some of the ambient noises from the surroundings to add to the soundtrack during editing. If your actors are supposed to be speaking in a busy restaurant, you will need to record the sounds of a crowded eatery. If the scene is played outdoors, the sounds of cars, airplanes overhead, or children's laughter will add a sense of realism.

Don't buy separate equipment for these noises; record them with your DV camcorder. Later, you can use them in the iMovie software as an audio track.

Composing Your Shots

Keeping a consistent style in your shots is critical. Make sure you are lighting every scene in a similar manner, always focusing your camera in similar ways and recording sounds at the same level. The camcorder will do most of these things consistently, but note any changes you make to the default settings so you create compositions that match when edited together.

Three Light Sources In this shot, you can see a main light source illuminates the actor's face and cast shadows on the lapel of his suit. A small light source on the floor is shielded by the actor's body; it shines patterns from the chair against the wall. A third light is part of the set décor (its reflection appears in the picture on the back wall) and gives dimension to the actor's head as well as diffusing harsh shadows around the wrinkles of his sleeve.

Extreme Angles The high point of action in the "First Impression" tutorial movie takes place when a skateboarder jumps into the air. For impact, the shot was composed from an extremely low angle, shooting skyward to silhouette the actor.

Composition is an artistic term describing the use of balance, proportion, and contrast to emphasize relationships between characters or objects in the frame. There are endless possibilities to composing shots, but a few guidelines can help.

Angles

Inventive camera angles can generate excitement in moving images. Try looking at your subjects from oblique viewpoints, finding a fresh perspective from which to shoot them. Become aware of these techniques in the films you admire and experiment wildly. Remember that extreme angles can be shocking to the viewer; for this reason use them only for highlights in the action or important story points. Overall, creative use of off-kilter shots is an excellent way to improve your image compositions.

Triangles

Elements in composition are sometimes referred to by their geometry, which is the basic shapes they suggest within the frame. Triangle compositions are common because they naturally create "directives," invisible lines of interest that seem to point the human eye toward the pivotal character or object in the scene. Another benefit of these compositions is their inherent scale, which magnifies the importance of one character by contrasting his side of the triangle with the sides of the opposing two characters.

Framing Within the Frame

Another way of drawing the eye to important characters or objects in the scene is to create a framing device (elements positioned next to each other that create borders like a picture frame) within the edges of the video image. This is effective because it helps show what the actors themselves are looking at, giving the audience a chance to see vicariously through the voyeuristic eyes of the characters.

Composition Reinforces Drama In this scene, the woman suddenly stops embracing the man, shifts to a position next to the bellhop, and the three faces create a triangle of interest within the frame. The offset balance of the shot, with two characters standing against one, heightens the sense of accusation.

Framing Within Shots You can isolate characters or objects within a scene, as the couple's bodies create a frame around the figure of the bellhop. This composition is equivalent to cutting to a medium shot of the bellhop but involves the audience through point of view.

chapter three
importing footage

Once you've recorded your precious footage on a digital camcorder, you can transfer it to your iMac DV computer by using iMovie's video capture features. This is simply the fastest way to get started; for once you import clips, you begin making movies. Getting footage from your camcorder to the computer is incredibly fast, and the Macintosh has been specifically designed to make this process easy. Both the camera and the iMac now have integrated technologies that speed the capture and encoding of digital video. In fact, it's so simple because there's only one way to get video footage into your iMac computer for use with the iMovie software—that's directly from the FireWire cable connected to your DV camcorder.

Once you import clips, you begin making movies.

Why FireWire Is So Hot

The iMac DV computer features a revolutionary high-speed data port for large file transfers and full-motion video capture. This serial input/output technology is officially called the IEEE 1394 standard, but its nickname is simply FireWire. First developed by Apple Computer, FireWire was designed to carry ultrafast data-rich digital signals to and from multimedia devices such as video camcorders. A host of other FireWire products, including disk drives, audio mixers, removable drives, DAT recorders, CD/DVD products, and printers are immediately compatible when connected to a Macintosh.

FireWire's rapid transformation of the computer peripherals industry is largely due to its amazing benefits. FireWire peripherals are "hot-pluggable," meaning you can disconnect and reconnect them without crashing your machine and without shutting off the computer's power. When a FireWire camcorder is "hot-plugged," the Macintosh will automatically recognize the connection, making the camcorder instantly ready to import your footage into iMovie.

 TIP

FIREWIRE FYI
IF YOUR CAMCORDER DOESN'T SAY FIREWIRE, DON'T FRET. APPLE'S PROTECTION OF THE PROPRIETARY NAME "FIREWIRE" HAS FORCED OTHER MANUFACTURERS TO COIN THEIR OWN TERMS. SONY USES THE NAME "I.LINK" ON MANY OF ITS DV CAMCORDERS. OTHERS SIMPLY USE THE GEEKY "IEEE 1394" TO ALLUDE TO THE INTERNATIONAL STANDARD FOR DEVICE COMPATIBILITY.

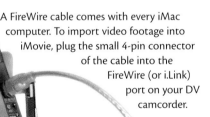

A FireWire cable comes with every iMac computer. To import video footage into iMovie, plug the small 4-pin connector of the cable into the FireWire (or i.Link) port on your DV camcorder.

The other end of the cable goes into the larger 6-pin ports on the side of your iMac. This cable can be connected or disconnected at any time, even while the computer is on.

There are some important distinctions. Although a Macintosh will normally support a "daisy-chain" of as many as 63 FireWire devices linked together, iMovie does not import footage from DV camcorders connected to such a chain. Nor does iMovie support the simultaneous use of multiple DV devices connected to your computer with FireWire. A single camcorder must be directly connected to the iMac computer by a single FireWire cable. Many FireWire peripherals don't require their own electrical source; they draw DC voltage from the computer's power supply. However, your iMac cannot power your DV camcorder; your camera must use a battery or AC outlet.

How Digital Video Works

When your camcorder records moving images, it quickly digitizes the millions of colors captured into a massive collection of data that describes how each color will be represented on every pixel of your television or computer monitor. In fact, much more color information is collected than will ever appear to the human eye, but it is necessary to capture a great deal of information to retain a high-quality image. This happens inside your camcorder, which is remarkably skillful at capturing clear images and recording them to magnetic tape. From this point, the digital video signal will remain "lossless," meaning it can survive repeated transfers from tape to tape, camcorder to camcorder, and computer to computer, without degrading the original image quality recorded by the camera.

When you transfer DV data from your camcorder to your computer using a FireWire connection, the computer does not have to digitize any of the video signal; it simply transfers the entire data segment for storage on your hard disk.

At no point will your iMovie software perform any function that jeopardizes the pristine quality of your footage. The DV format can survive as many as 1,000 transfers without any data loss. This benefit will become extremely important in Chapter 8, when you begin saving your movie for long-term storage.

Even when you apply titles or transitions to the DV footage and the images are rendered with special effects in iMovie, your footage is completely safe from any loss of quality. Only when iMovie is exporting back to tape—which requires iMovie to unlock the digital signal to combine the original source footage with the rendered effects—is the DV stream exposed to signal degradation. However, the losses in quality that may occur are minor enough to be deemed inconsequential.

> **USING THE SPACE BAR**
> THE SPACE BAR ON YOUR KEYBOARD IS A CONVENIENT SHORTCUT FOR STARTING AND STOPPING THE IMPORT OF DV FOOTAGE INTO IMOVIE IN CAPTURE MODE. WHEN YOU SWITCH TO THE PREVIEW MODE, THE SPACE BAR WILL ACT AS THE PLAY OR STOP BUTTON FOR VIEWING CLIPS.

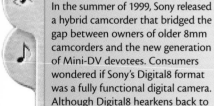

GETTING DIGITAL8 STRAIGHT

In the summer of 1999, Sony released a hybrid camcorder that bridged the gap between owners of older 8mm camcorders and the new generation of Mini-DV devotees. Consumers wondered if Sony's Digital8 format was a fully functional digital camera. Although Digital8 hearkens back to Sony's 8mm heritage, the new series of Digital8 Handycams are true digital camcorders that will work seamlessly with iMovie. Basically, the Digital8 Handycam series will connect to computers and other devices through a FireWire (IEEE 1394) port. Images acquired from standard 8mm or Hi8 tapes are first converted to a digital signal inside the camera before exporting to the iMovie. Digital8 cameras don't use the popular MiniDV cassettes to record but save digital sound and images on standard 8mm or Hi8 tapes. They can also play older 8mm or Hi8 analog cassettes. Technically, all of your iMovie footage can be saved to the Digital8 8mm and Hi8 formats, but make sure to use metal-particle Hi8 tapes to reduce artifacts that can appear when digital recordings are displayed over analog playback devices.

Importing Clips into iMovie

You'll want to open a new project in iMovie before you begin importing new footage into the computer. At the very moment you connect a DV device to the iMac computer, iMovie will detect the device and switch the Preview Window to Capture Mode. You can also do this manually by clicking the Capture Mode button located to the left of the Controller.

Is the Camera Connected?

FireWire sends more than merely footage to your computer—it sends a host of information regarding the status of your camcorder and its footage. Due to this exchange of information, your iMac can immediately sense when your camcorder has been connected or disconnected. Once you've plugged in the FireWire cable, iMovie can instantly tell when a videotape has been loaded or unloaded. Any time a change in your camcorder operations takes place, status messages will be updated in the center of the screen against a blue background. Make sure you don't unplug your DV device during the import process.

Complete Control of Your Camcorder

FireWire's unique properties even allow the iMovie software to operate the main controls of your DV camcorder from inside the application. This feature is extremely convenient for moviemakers because it does not require you to push the tiny buttons on your compact camcorder when searching for footage. The on-screen buttons of the Controller will work as a remote control for the common operations of record, play, rewind, forward, and pause. This is ideal for searching, capturing, and displaying footage from your Mini-DV camcorder.

Selecting Footage for Import

With the Controller buttons, you can locate the exact footage you wish to import and begin capturing the scene by pressing the large Import button just above the Controller. Immediately, iMovie creates an icon in the Clip Shelf and the duration value counts the time of the footage as it is being transferred to

Remote Control On-screen buttons provide remote control of record, play, rewind, forward, and pause features. The Import button begins the capture of new footage—you can even activate it while the video is playing at full motion.

CAPTURE MODE   VIEW MODE

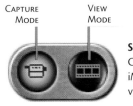

Set to Import When the Capture button is highlighted, iMovie is ready to import your video footage.

your computer's hard disk. The frames of the captured footage will appear in the Preview Window. When you have captured all of the footage you need, press the Import button again to stop the capture. You can also use the Stop or Pause button to end a capture session.

Batch Capturing by Timecode

To capture several clips at once, or the entire contents of your videotape, you'll need to set the iMovie preferences to automatically separate sequences by their unique timecode values. Once these preferences are changed, iMovie will transfer the high-quality video into the program, breaking footage into individual clips by the gaps between the date/time information that is embedded in the digital video signal. For example, if you recorded a few minutes of your son's soccer match and then later recorded his postgame reactions, iMovie will detect a disparity in the timecode and snip the scene into two clips. It's convenient.

Maximum Length for Captured Footage

The maximum length of a movie is limited only by the available disk space on your computer. There is no limit to the number of clips that can be combined to create a single movie. However, the maximum file size of an individual movie clip is 2 gigabytes. If you exceed this 2-gigabyte limit during an extended duration capture, iMovie will continue the capture as a second clip.

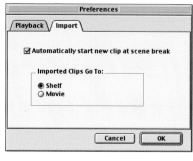

Preference Settings Changing the import preferences will allow you to batch capture and separate long stretches of footage by their timecode values. You can also determine whether imported clips are placed in the clip shelf or directly into the timeline.

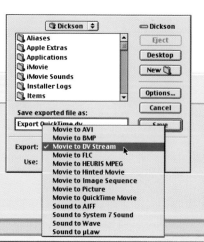

No QuickTime Import?

Unfortunately, iMovie will not (easily) allow the import of DV footage from any source other than direct capture from a FireWire device. No other movie files, including Apple's own popular QuickTime format, are officially supported. However, there is a workaround. With the $30 QuickTime Pro authoring upgrade, you can export movie files in the DV Stream format and drop them into the Media folder of your iMovie projects. When you open the project, a dialog box will prompt you to trash the unexpected files. Simply respond by clicking the "Leave Them Alone" button, and the QuickTime files will appear in the Clip Shelf, ready for use.

Capturing Live Video from a Camera

In some cases, your digital camcorder may allow you to record images directly to the computer hard disk—even when there is no tape in the camera. This is handy when you are recording in close proximity to your iMac DV and wish to expedite the moviemaking process by capturing video "live." To capture live video from a camera, switch your camcorder to Camera mode and set the Lock/Standby switch to Standby. Remove any cassettes in the camera. (A tape in the camera will cause the camera to time out and go into sleep mode.) If the camera requires a tape to be in it but does not play video through to iMovie, check that the tape's write protection tab is unlocked. One other thing: Make sure the camera's demo mode is disabled. (Some cameras switch to a demo mode when left on standby without a tape inserted.) Check for a demo function in your camcorder's settings menu, and disable it.

When Space Runs Out

As you continue to import video footage, the free space indicator will estimate the amount of capture capacity left on local hard disks. When disk space runs out, or when no more empty spaces are available on the Clip Shelf, a dialog box will appear, prompting you to move some clips to the timeline. Do not attempt to capture video to projects saved on a remote server or to storage devices that reside over a network; the variable speeds of these networks cannot sustain the proper data rate for video capture.

Free Space A status bar on the iMovie interface indicates the amount of free hard disk space available for the capture of DV footage.

Renaming Clips

You can rename any of the clips imported into iMovie quickly by selecting the icon in the Clip Shelf. After the clip name is highlighted in blue, begin typing on your keyboard. The new name will appear at the bottom of clip (the name will be 10 to 26 letters long, depending largely upon the width of characters).

Deleting Clips

To remove a clip from the timeline or the Clip Shelf, simply highlight the clip and press the Delete key on your keyboard. You can also use the Clear command in the Edit menu. To restore deleted clips, choose the Undo command from the Edit menu (or use the Command-Z keyboard shortcut). If you empty the Trash in iMovie, you will not be able to undo any actions taken prior to emptying the Trash. **Clips cannot be restored after the project has been saved.**

CONVERTING ANALOG VIDEO TO DIGITAL

The Achilles' heel of DV has been its poor integration with analog devices. So a product such as Sony's $500 DVMC-DA1 Media Converter is a godsend. It converts incoming analog audio and video into a DV-compressed digital stream *and* exports digital signals to analog devices.

Better yet, it allows for input and output of both signals through its FireWire, Composite, or S-Video jacks. But the magic of the DVMC-DA1 is its ability to capture analog video streams and convert to DV format in real-time as it sends digital sounds and images to your iMac

over FireWire. This clever box makes analog footage appear as higher-resolution data. Once this footage is converted into a digital video signal, it can be recorded to a Mini-DV tape, uploaded to a computer with a FireWire connection, or accessed by a digital camcorder.

Viewing Your Footage

You can preview your captured clips by setting the monitor to Preview Mode and double-clicking the icon in the Clip Shelf. You can also watch the clip in full-screen, although the image may appear slightly pixelated at this size. Despite the choppy playback displayed in the full screen mode, iMovie maintains your video footage in pristine quality and keeps audio in perfect sync.

View Mode Once you have finished capturing your DV footage, switch to the View mode to preview or edit clips.

HOW COME MY FOOTAGE LOOKS BLOCKY?

When the Macintosh imports DV footage, it keeps the original pristine source files on the hard disk and creates a series of preview frames to display in the iMovie application. These preview frames are created by removing much of the video and color information that NTSC televi- sions require and simply displaying the frames as they will best appear on your computer monitor. Don't worry, though. The screen images you see are only lower-resolution stand-ins for use in viewing your results in iMovie. These preview frames will display quicker at full screen and full-motion than the higher-resolution images.

chapter four

cropping clips

In iMovie development circles, a favorite saying was, "Edit is a four-letter word." Consumer focus groups feared that editing required a level of skill and knowledge beyond their grasp. Apple's software engineers and marketing executives agreed to do more than avoid the use of technical jargon; they designed the iMovie software to keep the process simple. By Apple's design, the application has the wonderful ability to calm all apprehensions. To help you stay calm, let's demystify the entire editing cycle. The act of "cropping" video clips is nothing more than the removal of unnecessary footage. If a more soothing phrase such as "trimming away the fat" or "selecting the best moments" will help you overcome any trepidation, feel free to substitute the term throughout this chapter. But there's really no trick to cropping footage, as the following lesson will assure you.

Edit is a four-letter word.

Viewing Clips

Although there are two ways of viewing clips in iMovie, the Eye-View Timeline is the better choice for cropping clips because it provides you with the same icons that you will be working with in the Clip Shelf.

To make the Eye-View Timeline the active window, click the graphic of the eye in the tabs at the bottom left corner of the iMovie interface.

The clip duration is displayed in the upper left-hand corner of the icon. iMovie calculates time values by dividing video into 30 frames for every second. The value 49:06 indicates a duration of 49 seconds and 6 frames. The position of the playhead appears in the icon as a red line; this line moves along the based of the icon as the clip is played.

Selecting Clips for Preview

In preparing to crop footage, you'll need to switch into Preview Mode by clicking the Clip View button located just below the controller. You can also accomplish this by selecting any of the clips in the Timeline or Clip Shelf.

Once you've selected a clip, a yellow highlight will appear around its borders. The duration of the footage appears in the upper left-hand corner of the icon. You can then manipulate these highlighted clips from either the Timeline or the Clip Shelf. You can duplicate them by using the Copy and Paste features of the Macintosh. You can delete them simply by

TIP

RESTORING DELETED CLIPS
CLIPS THAT HAVE BEEN ACCIDENTLY DELETED CAN BE RESTORED, THANKS TO IMOVIE'S UNLIMITED UNDO. SIMPLY SELECT UNDO FROM THE EDIT MENU OR USE THE KEYBOARD COMMAND-Z.

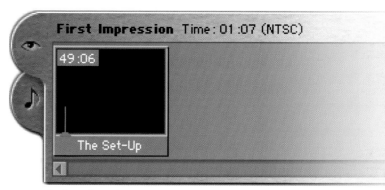

Viewing Clips The Eye-View Timeline displays the name and duration of your movie project. To activate this view, click the "eye" icon in the upper left-hand corner of the timeline.

HOW TIME IS DISPLAYED IN iMOVIE

In the timeline view, the total duration of your movie will be displayed above the clips, in the titlebar header of the timeline. This duration will be expressed in hours:minutes:seconds only. No frames are indicated in the timeline header.

However, the duration of clips in iMovie is expressed as minutes: seconds:frames. For example, longer clips may appear with the value 01:07:13, indicating 1 minute, 7 seconds, and 13 frames. iMovie can express hours as well, but it is unlikely

(and not recommended) that you should capture footage in such large increments.

When viewing footage one frame at a time, you will notice that the duration value changes after the 29th frame in any clip. That's because

digital video is recorded at 30 frames per second, beginning with the value :00. So, if you are viewing a frame at 21:29 (or the 21st second, 29th frame) the very next frame will be expressed as 22:00.

pressing the delete key (you can also use the Clear command from the Edit menu). You can restore them easily and endlessly—because iMovie allows unlimited levels of Undo. You can also move icons into the timeline below the Clip Shelf by dragging the icon to any position in the Eye-View Timeline window.

There may be times when you want to remove a clip from the timeline but save it for future use. In this case, it's best to return a clip from the timeline to the Clip Shelf. You can do this simply by dragging the icon over an empty space in the Clip Shelf. If you have selected multiple icons they will be placed in empty spaces on the Clip Shelf in the order in which they were selected. When you attempt to return more timeline clips than the Clip Shelf has empty spaces for, the icons will simply return to the timeline.

Time Markers Using the Clip Markers

When you've selected an icon in the EyeView Timeline or the Clip Shelf, iMovie will immediately activate the Preview Window and display the first frame of the clip. The Preview Window will also include time markers beneath the footage as well as display the position of the playhead. As you use the controller buttons to play clips, the playhead will move steadily across the time markers to indicate the exact frame that appears above.

These time markers are essential for cropping clips, because they are used to place the crop sliders in position before extracting unwanted footage. With your cursor, you can individually move your crop sliders. With the keys on your keyboard, you can move incrementally from frame to frame to place crop sliders on specific time markers.

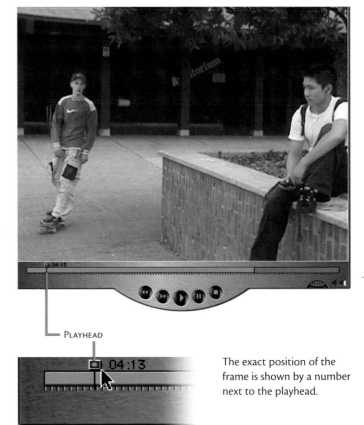

PLAYHEAD

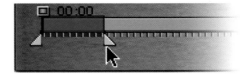

The exact position of the frame is shown by a number next to the playhead.

Crop sliders are activated by dragging your cursor along the time markers.

USING ARROW KEYS

DRAGGING THE PLAYHEAD OR CROP SLIDERS CAN BE DIFFICULT WHEN YOU ARE ATTEMPTING TO MOVE CLIPS IN SMALL INCREMENTS. YOU CAN ACCOMPLISH THIS MORE EASILY BY USING THE RIGHT AND LEFT ARROW KEYS ON YOUR KEYBOARD, WHICH WILL MOVE THE CLIP FORWARD OR BACKWARD ONE FRAME AT A TIME.

Lesson: First Impression

In this lesson, you will use raw video clips of a movie to discover how footage can be cropped, split, and cleared in iMovie. You'll create a sequence of actions that, once combined, give the illusion of fluid movement. This group of clips features a skateboarder's attempt to perform difficult stunts. (In some cases, the actor makes several attempts in the same clip.) Trim each clip to its essential action so that when joined together as a series of shots, the skateboarder appears to have executed the entire stunt without a flaw.

A sample of the finished movie, "First Impression.mov," can be found in the QuickTime Gallery folder on the DVD-ROM disc.

Step One: Cropping out Unnecessary Footage

With the iMovie application launched, you can begin this lesson by opening the project called "First Impression."

1 Choose Open Project from the File Menu.

▼ **2** Locate the "Cropping Clips" Folder and select the "First Impression" project. When the "First Impression" project is open, the Clip Shelf will display nine icons. You will crop these unedited video clips.

Stunt 1

Stunt 2

Stunt 3

Stunt 4

Stunt 5

Stunt 6

Stunt 7

Stunt 8

Final Scene

First Impression Time: 01:07 (NTSC)

49:06

The Set-Up

◀ **3** A single clip will appear in the timeline. With the Eye-View Timeline showing, highlight the clip labeled "The Set-Up" with your cursor, position the playhead at the start of the Preview Window, and press the Play button in the Preview controls. This opening scene introduces the action sequence you are about to create.

04:06

Stunt 1

◀ **4** Next, select the icon in the Clip Shelf labeled "Stunt 1." A yellow highlight will appear around the edges of the icon to indicate that the clip has been selected. The first frame of the clip will also appear in the Preview Window.

00:00

◀ **5** Position the playhead at the beginning of the clip markers, and drag your cursor just below the playhead to activate the crop sliders. As you drag the triangular crop sliders, a dark blue area will indicate the frames that you are selecting. The playhead will snap into the position when the slider stops, displaying the time at that marker.

View the clip "Stunt 1," and note how the actor stumbles off the skateboard near the end of the clip. By removing this portion of the footage, we can match it with the subsequent clips to make it appear as though the actor gracefully continues the ride.

You can use the arrow keys on your keyboard to move the sliders (in either direction) one frame at a time.

◀ **6** Leave the left crop slider at the 00:00 position, and drag the right slider until the playhead falls at the 02:16 time marker. The Preview frame should look like the picture to the left.

◀ **7** Once your crop sliders are set, choose the Crop command from the Edit menu.

◀ **8** The duration of the "Stunt 1" icon in the Clip Shelf should now read 02:16. If you have made a mistake, choose Undo from the Edit menu and try again.

◀ **9** To crop the next clip, select the icon labeled "Stunt 2" in the Clip Shelf.

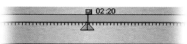

Notice how the posture of the actor in this frame, particularly his arms, are similar to the last frame in the clip "Stunt 1." This visual similarity will help connect the actions of these clips when they are viewed together.

◀ **10** Next, you will need to set the playhead to 02:20 and click the time marker to activate your crop sliders. The frame should correspond to the picture to the left.

◀ **11** Leaving the left slider at 02:20, drag the right slider until the playhead reads 04:15. If the Preview frame matches the picture to the left, choose Crop from the Edit menu (or use the keyboard shortcut Command-K).

◀ **12** The duration of the "Stunt 2" icon in the Clip Shelf should now read 01:25. If not, choose Undo from the Edit menu (or use the keyboard shortcut Command-Z) and try again.

◀ **13** Next, highlight the icon labeled "Stunt 3" in the Clip Shelf and play the clip in the Preview Window. Although the actor attempts to make a jump twice, only a portion of his initial attempt will be required for the sequence.

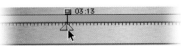

14 To crop the clip, set the playhead at 03:13 and click the time marker to activate your crop sliders. The frame should correspond to the picture to the left.

15 Leaving the left slider at 03:13, drag the right slider until the playhead reads 03:24. If the Preview frame matches the picture to the left, crop the selection.

DRAGGING MULTIPLE CLIPS

TO SELECT MULTIPLE CLIPS AT ONCE, HOLD YOUR SHIFT KEY DOWN AS YOU SELECT ICONS WITH YOUR CURSOR. THE ORDER IN WHICH YOU SELECT CLIPS WILL DETERMINE THE ORDER OF THEIR PLACEMENT IN A SEQUENCE WHEN DRAGGED INTO THE TIMELINE.

16 The duration of the "Stunt 3" icon should now read 00:10, indicating 10 frames.

Step Two: Putting Clips into the Timeline

The timeline can hold an unlimited number of clips, but the Clip Shelf is limited to the empty spaces available. Sometimes, it's necessary to drag clips into the timeline to clear additional space on the Clip Shelf. This is a good idea when you are about to import additional footage, duplicate icons, or split footage into two clips. You can drag icons individually into the time-line or select several clips and drag an entire sequence into the timeline at once.

▲ **1** With the "First Impression" project still open, highlight the "Stunt 1" icon by selecting it with your cursor. Then, holding down the Shift key on your keyboard, select the "Stunt 2" and "Stunt 3" icons until all three are high-lighted. (You can also accomplish this by dragging your cursor across the entire row, creating a selection box around the perimeter of the icons in the Clip Shelf.)

▲ **2** Once the icons are selected, drag them together as a group into the timeline and place them after the first icon, "The Set-Up." A ghosted box will indicate where your selection will be placed.

![49:06 timeline bar]

▲ **3** If the icons are still highlighted, the Preview Window will display all of the clips. Position the playhead at the beginning of the first clip and select Play to watch your cropped clips together in a sequence.

◀ **4** Let's resume cropping the other clips. Highlight the icon labeled "Stunt 4" in the Clip Shelf.

◀ **5** Position the left slider at 01:00, and drag the right slider until the playhead reads 01:10. If the Preview frames match the picture to the left, choose Crop from the Edit menu.

◀ **6** Highlight the icon labeled "Stunt 5" in the Clip Shelf.

◀ **7** Position the left slider at 06:04, and drag the right slider until the playhead reads 08:08. Check to see that the Preview frames match the pictures above, and crop the clip.

◀ **8** The duration of the "Stunt 5" icon should now read 02:04.

Step Three: Splitting One Clip into Two

In many action sequences, it is better to split a clip into two parts, allowing you (the director) to suspend certain moments by "cutting away" to another viewpoint, action, or reaction. In this skateboarding stunt, the same action was shot from several angles. By splitting Stunt 5 into two parts, you can interrupt the action momentarily by showing a different angle of the ride before returning to the original view.

1 With the "Stunt 1" clip icon still selected, set the playhead to the 01:00 time marker, and choose the Split Clip at Playhead command from the Edit menu. (You can also use the keyboard shortcut Command-T for this operation.)

2 iMovie will split the clip into two parts and create another icon in the Clip Shelf, using the title "Stunt 5/1" to indicate the connection between these clips. Both clips will remain highlighted until you select another element with your cursor.

3 Leave the split clip icons in the Clip Shelf for a moment, and continue cropping the "Stunt 6" clip by highlighting it with your cursor.

4 Set the crop sliders at 01:00 and 02:22, and crop the "Stunt 6" clip. The duration of the "Stunt 6" icon should read 01:22.

▲ **5** Select the "Stunt 4," "Stunt 5," "Stunt 5/1," and "Stunt 6" icons in the Clip Shelf, and drag them as a group into the timeline. Place them at the end, to the right of the "Stunt 3" icon.

6 Deselect the icons by clicking anywhere in the timeline header or titlebar area. You can also deselect the icons by choosing Select None in the Edit menu (or by using the keyboard shortcut Command-D).

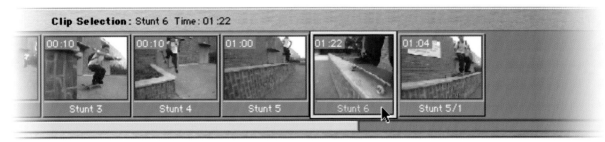

▲ **7** Now, you can highlight just the icon "Stunt 6" and drag it to the left before placing it between the "Stunt 5" and "Stunt 5/1" icons in the sequence. You'll notice how the icons move aside to show where the icon will be placed when you let go of the mouse button.

8 Deselect the icon (by choosing Select None in the Edit menu, using the keyboard shortcut Command-D, or clicking anywhere in the timeline header or titlebar area), drag the playhead in the Preview Window to the starting position, and press the Play button to watch the sequence in motion.

Step Four: Cropping Clips in the Timeline

It's quite logical for the organized moviemaker to want to crop footage in the Clip Shelf and move it into the timeline as each is completed (as you've done in the lesson so far). However, occasionally it becomes necessary to monitor the flow of action across several clips, and this may require you to drag icons into the timeline *before* you crop them. As our skateboarding sequence evolves, let's see how unedited clips can be trimmed from the timeline.

▲ **1** Select the icons for "Stunt 7" and "Stunt 8," and drag the clips into the timeline, placing them behind the last icon in the sequence (the one labeled "Stunt 5/1").

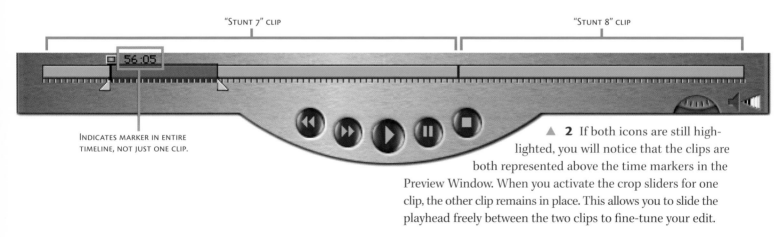

"STUNT 7" CLIP

"STUNT 8" CLIP

INDICATES MARKER IN ENTIRE TIMELINE, NOT JUST ONE CLIP.

▲ **2** If both icons are still highlighted, you will notice that the clips are both represented above the time markers in the Preview Window. When you activate the crop sliders for one clip, the other clip remains in place. This allows you to slide the playhead freely between the two clips to fine-tune your edit.

▲ **3** Notice how the time markers express a different value than the icons in the Clip Shelf. Since you are cropping clips from the Timeline, the markers will indicate the length of the entire time-line. So, you must set the crop sliders at 56:05 and 57:03 to crop the "Stunt 7" clip.

ONCE CROPPED, THE "STUNT 7" CLIP APPEARS SMALLER IN TIMELINE.

PROPORTIONALLY, THE "STUNT 8" CLIP WILL APPEAR BIGGER.

▲ **4** You should also notice how the Preview Window instantly makes an adjustment for the length of the clip indicated by the time markers. Now you can crop "Stunt 8."

CROPS THAT STRADDLE CLIPS
ANOTHER EFFICIENT WAY TO CROP CLIPS IS TO REMOVE FOOTAGE FROM TWO ADJACENT CLIPS AT ONCE. TO DO THIS, SIMPLY SELECT TWO CLIPS AT ONCE (BY HOLDING DOWN THE SHIFT KEY AS YOU CLICK ICONS) AND ONCE THE CLIPS APPEAR IN THE MONITOR, DRAG THE CROP SLIDERS SO THAT THEY STRADDLE THE FRAMES ON BOTH CLIPS. ONCE THIS IS DONE, SELECT THE CROP OR CLEAR COMMAND TO DELETE THE UNWANTED FOOTAGE.

▲ **5** Set the crop sliders at 58:01 and 58:19, and crop the "Stunt 8" clip.

6 The duratin of the clips should now read 00:28 and 00:18 respectively.

Step Five: Clearing Footage from a Clip

At times, you'll simply want to remove a short bit from the middle of a very long clip—without having to make two separate crops. This can be done more conveniently with the Clear command. Unlike the Crop command (which removes all footage outside of the crop markers), the Clear command removes the footage that resides within the crop markers.

◀ **1** Select the last clip, "Final Scene." Leave the icon in the Clip Shelf, and continue cropping the "Stunt 6" clip by highlighting it with your cursor.

◀ **2** Position the left crop slider at 05:18, and drag the right slider until the playhead reads 07:02. Make sure the Preview frames match the pictures above.

▲ **3** Choose the Clear command from the Edit menu.

▲ **4** iMovie will split the clip into two icons. Notice how the combined durations of the clips are exactly 14 frames less than the original single clip.

First Impression Time: 01:07 (NTSC)

| 01:04 | 00:28 | 00:18 | 05:18 | 01:27 |
| Stunt 5/1 | Stunt 7 | Stunt 8 | Final Scene | Final Scene/1 |

▲ **5** Position the left slider at 01:00, and drag the right slider until the playhead reads 01:10. If the Preview frames match the pictures above, choose Crop from the Edit menu.

Before You Save

Computer users have grown accustomed to saving their documents frequently throughout the course of a project. However, the iMovie software, which manages large files taking up generous portions of hard disk space, will immediately look for opportunities to get rid of unused footage after you use the Save command. In most cases, this is what you want. But a word of caution: the Undo feature—the command that enables you to reclaim cropped footage or reassemble split clips—is rendered useless the moment the Save command is executed.

Puns aside, the Save command in iMovie can be a double-edged sword. Saving your project periodically will eliminate your chances of stepping back to experiment with alternative editing decisions. However, by not saving your work frequently, you run the risk of losing your hard-earned steps during power outages or system crashes.

Confirm Save

You have made changes to your project 'First Impression' that have not been saved. Would you like to save them?

[Don't Save] [Cancel] [Save]

Ready to Save? Unlike other applications, the Save command in iMovie will render the Undo feature useless—which means you can't reclaim cropped footage or reassemble split clips. So make sure you are satisfied with your project before saving.

chapter five
adding sound and music

An important part of any movie is the soundtrack. You'll soon discover—through the addition of sound effects, music, and narration—that audio is the most powerful and dynamic aspect to storytelling. You have several ways to bring audio into the iMovie application. Although there are limits to the kinds of audio files you can import, there is no limit to the amount of clips you can include. This opens up great opportunities for moviemakers who want to enrich their stories with the depth and complexity a good soundtrack can provide. In fact, first-time directors using iMovie may never know how easy they have it. Previously, digital audio was recorded on a separate system from the film camera equipment (usually DAT tape) at a different rate of speed. This made reliable synchronization tough for the filmmaker. Fortunately, this concern has been eliminated by the digital video (DV) format.

Audio is the most powerful and dynamic aspect to storytelling.

Audio in Perfect Sync

The DV format—which is what's used in most commercial camcorders today—keeps audio completely synchronized with the moving images at all times. Furthermore, once the digital video footage is encoded and transferred to your computer, the audio and video travel together through the entire production cycle. More sophisticated video applications allow you to extract the soundtrack from its accompanying video image, but iMovie forbids this practice.

Currently, there are only a few choices for playback of the synchronized audio attached to your captured footage. You can turn the volume off completely, turn it up completely, or adjust it somewhere in between. The benefit of this is that your characters' dialogue is always in sync with the picture. However, this makes it tough to overlap a single line of dialogue with several different images.

Selecting Sounds in the Audio Timeline

Sound files in iMovie are displayed in the Audio Timeline viewer, which can be activated by clicking the tab under the Clip Viewer—the tab has an icon of a musical note. The Audio Timeline includes three separate representations of audio. The synchronized sound in video footage is displayed as blue clips on the top bar. The middle bar shows audio files introduced

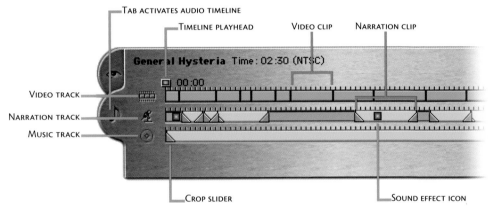

TAB ACTIVATES AUDIO TIMELINE
TIMELINE PLAYHEAD
VIDEO CLIP
NARRATION CLIP

General Hysteria Time: 02:30 (NTSC)

□ 00:00

VIDEO TRACK
NARRATION TRACK
MUSIC TRACK

CROP SLIDER
SOUND EFFECT ICON

TIP

SELECTING MULTIPLE CLIPS
YOU CAN SELECT SEVERAL AUDIO CLIPS AT ONCE (TO MAKE SIMILAR ADJUSTMENTS IN VOLUME OR FADE SETTINGS) BY HOLDING DOWN THE SHIFT KEY WHILE CLICKING CLIPS IN THE TIMELINE.

Audio files share many of the same properties of video clips; they can easily be cropped, shuffled, duplicated, or deleted from the timeline. Audio clips can also overlap, letting you combine several sound effects for added impact.

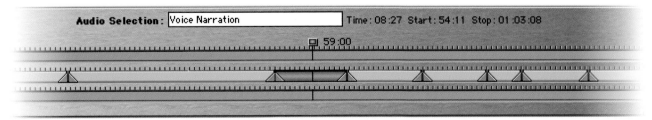

Audio Selection: Voice Narration   Time: 08:27 Start: 54:11 Stop: 01:03:08

□ 59:00

Audio clips will change color when they are selected. Once highlighted, a clip's volume and time markers will change immediately to indicate their precise position and duration.

into the timeline through the Sounds palette, particularly sound effects and narration clips. The bottom bar indicates music tracks captured from CD-ROM discs through the Music palette as well as audio files imported into iMovie using the File menu's Import Command.

The timeline also has an Audio Selection readout in the top center, which will display the current name and duration of any clip once it is selected. This information includes the starting point of the audio clip as well as the marker location where the file stops. You can change the name of any clip by highlighting the text in the Audio Selection box and typing in a replacement.

The number of audio files and sound effects is limited only by the capacity of your iMac computer. Although the interface may become a bit unruly, the possibilities are endless; you may overlap audio files on top of one another or duplicate the same sound again and again. This flexibility lets you experiment with a wide range of creative sound options.

Changing the Audio Settings

When you've got lots of sound edits to make, you may want to isolate one track to hear it more clearly. iMovie lets you turn off audio tracks to listen to sounds without interference from other tracks. Turning audio tracks off is relatively easy. Simply click the checkbox at the end of an audio track to mute all of the clips on that track (a checkmark in the box indicates that the track is active; an empty box means it's mute). It's important to understand that muted tracks will not be included in the soundtrack of your final movie if you do not reactivate them before exporting to a QuickTime file or videotape.

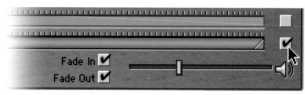

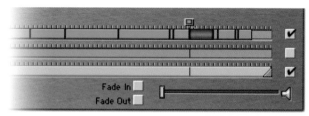

To temporarily turn off an audio track, uncheck the checkbox. This prevents all sounds on the track from playing anywhere along the timeline.

To change the volume of audio files, simply select a clip in the Audio Viewer and move the volume slider in the bottom-right corner of the timeline.

TIP

MASTER VOLUME

BEYOND ADJUSTMENTS FOR INDIVIDUAL CLIPS, THERE ARE TWO WAYS TO ADJUST THE MASTER VOLUME LEVEL IN iMOVIE. MASTER VOLUME CAN BE SET BY DRAGGING THE THUMBWHEEL AT THE BOTTOM RIGHT-HAND CORNER OF THE MONITOR PREVIEW WINDOW. YOU CAN ALSO PRESS THE UP AND DOWN ARROW KEYS ON YOUR KEYBOARD TO CONTROL VOLUME.

After working with multiple audio clips, you may discover that the recording levels of certain sounds may be too loud or may interfere with the clarity of another clip. In these cases, it often helps to vary the volume levels of each file independently. The volume slider, located at the bottom right hand corner of the timeline, allows you to set the desired level for any audio clip; this applies to video clips, narration, sound effects, music, and imported audio files. Each audio file may be adjusted individually, but there can be only one setting for the entire duration of the clip. *Volume levels cannot fluctuate within the same clip.*

However, it is possible to have your clips fade in gradually and diminish smoothly as they come to an end. Fading audio is accomplished by clicking the Fade In and Fade Out checkboxes located to the left of the volume slider. The degree to which clips fade (both in and out) is calculated by the iMovie application, and there are no user controls to alter this effect. As with volume adjustments, these settings can be applied to individual clips or to multiple clips selected as a group. You can select a group of clips by holding down the Shift key and clicking them. Each type of sound file will change its appearance to indicate a selection; the video clips turn deep blue, narration and music will appear as a darker orange, and the sound effects are highlighted around the edges of their red squares.

Selecting from the Sound Effects Collection

A variety of prerecorded sound effects comes installed with iMovie. This collection includes everything from simple noises such as birdcalls and musical instruments to more elaborate and professional effects such as audience laugh tracks and studio applause. You can easily add these sound effects to your projects by dragging them into the Audio timeline from the Sounds palette.

Selecting Sounds
Special effects such as the Crowd Clapping file can be instantly added to your soundtrack by dragging clips from Sounds palette to the timeline.

Lesson: The Flower of Love

This lesson will demonstrate the basic application of audio to your movie projects. The first steps will use the middle track in the Audio timeline to show how sound effects and narration can be used to enhance your storyline. To save time, the music track has already been recorded and placed into the timeline to establish the duration of the project. Also, the synchronized audio portions of the footage clips in the top track have been preset. You can examine these settings by selecting any clip and viewing the volume slider and fade controls.

DVD To complete this lesson, you will need to move the Adding Sound folder from the DVD-ROM disc to the hard disk of your iMac DV computer. If you do not have enough space to hold all of the files necessary for this chapter, you may wish to remove the lesson folder from the previous chapter. Several other sample movies on the disc will help illustrate these audio principles; they can be found in the "Flower of Love.mov" file in the QuickTime Gallery folder.

Step One: Adding Sound Effects to the Timeline

With the iMovie application launched, you can begin this lesson by opening the project called "Flower of Love."

1 Choose Open Project from the File Menu.

2 Locate the Adding Sound folder, and select the "Flower of Love" project. Once the project is open, click the Audio Viewer tab to see the three tracks in the timeline. Note that the Music track at the bottom of the timeline has been unchecked to temporarily mute the track. Drag the playhead to the leftmost position, and play the movie (either by pressing your Space bar or by clicking the Play controller button in the Preview window).

This is how the movie sounds with only the synchronized video track activated.

3 Now, click the checkbox at the end of the Music track to hear how the instrumental score lends a dramatic tone to the movie.

4 Next, click the Sounds button to open the Sounds palette.

▼ 5 Locate the sound effect called "Man's Knock" from the list in the Sounds palette, and click it once. You will hear the sound effect.

6 Drag the "Woman's Knock" sound from the list, and position it on the middle track of the Audio timeline.

7 Using your cursor, drag the red square until the playhead indicates the position of 30:01 in the timeline. Use your arrow keys to move the clip a frame at a time.

To hear the sound effect clip while watching your movie in the monitor, drag the playhead in the audio viewer to a position preceding the sound effect clip and press the Space bar.

8 From the Sounds palette, locate the clip called "Man's Knock" and drag it from the list into the middle track of the Audio timeline.

▼ **9** Place the clip at the position of 01:01:05 in the timeline. Move the playhead to the left of the clip, and press the Space bar to hear the effect.

10 Next, duplicate the "Man's Knock" sound effect by selecting the red square in the timeline and choosing the Copy and Paste commands in the Edit menu.

Make sure the blue highlight appears around the edges of the red square to indicate that the clip is selected. You can use the keyboard shortcuts Command-C for copy and Command-V to paste the sound effect.

DELETING SOUND EFFECTS

You can delete any sound or music file by highlighting it in the Audio Timeline and pressing the Delete key (or choosing the Clear command in the Edit menu). If you would like to restore a deleted audio clip, simply choose Undo from the Edit menu (or use the keyboard shortcut Command-Z). You can repeat the Undo command several times to restore many of your previous steps.

▼ **11** Place the duplicated clip at the position of 01:50:12 in the timeline. Move the playhead to the left, and press the Space bar to hear it.

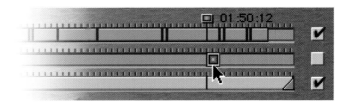

12 Locate the clip called "Bags for 213" from the Sounds palette, and drag it into the middle track of the Audio timeline.

▼ **13** Place the clip at the position of 01:02:25 in the timeline.

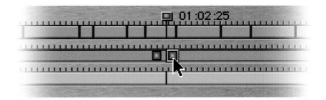

At this point, you can play the movie from the beginning to get a sense of the impact that the sound effects will have on your finished story. Some sounds are vital, providing missing information or dialogue from characters that cannot be seen. Sound effects also help work as cues—audio that motivates an action. In this sequence, the first knock at the door prompts the actor to turn around, the second knock makes him open his eyes and look toward the door. The announcement of the bellhop also initiates a response from the actress. Even the last knock, presented during the titles, informs the audience that the movie is not quite over yet. These sound effects each serve to move the narrative forward and send the story into its next action.

Now, you can add some prerecorded narration clips that feature the actors delivering supplemental dialogue in voiceovers.

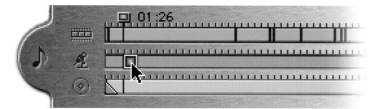

▲ **14** Locate the clip called "Narration #1" from the Sounds palette, drag it into the middle audio track, and place it at the position of 01:26 in the timeline. Remember to use the arrow keys for precise placement of the playhead.

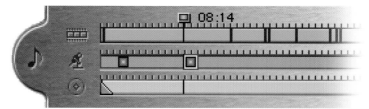

▲ **15** Next, locate the clip called "Narration #2" from the Sounds palette, and drag it to the position of 08:14 in the timeline.

16 Now, locate the clip called "Narration #3" from the Sounds palette, drag it to the position of 12:17 in the timeline.

After you have finished, drag the playhead to the beginning of the timeline and press the Space bar to listen to the three narration clips.

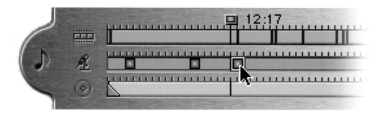

Using Narration

Narration adds an extended viewpoint to storytelling—one that can be deeply psychological. The voiceover can appear removed and objective—as in a documentary or news coverage. It can also be subjective, exposing a personal stake a character might have in the action. In many cases, the narrator is a character who is not a visible participant, such as a guardian angel or puppetmaster who oversees the events and simply reports on them. However, narration is more commonly used to fortify the point of view of the main characters, delivering insight into their thoughts in much the same way that the camera records what they are seeing.

Your iMac DV computer is well equipped for recording voiceover narrations. It contains a built-in microphone; however, you can also use an external microphone if you prefer. Once you've activated the Sounds palette (or plugged a microphone into the audio input jack), you can capture narration and import it as a clip directly into the middle audio track on the timeline.

USING YOUR MICROPHONE WITH iMOVIE

Your iMac comes with a built-in microphone, centered just over the top of the screen. This sensor is highly sensitive, having the ability to record sounds within a CD-quality bandwidth of 44.100 kHz. It is powerful enough to pick up sounds within a range of several feet. To use the built-in microphone as the sound input device, you'll need to access the Sound control panel from the Apple menu.

With the Sound control panel open, click the Sound button and choose the Built-in Mic setting from the Sound Monitoring Source pop-up menu. (You can also access these settings from the Control Strip on your desktop.)

The iMac DV models also accept another sound-in source; the Apple PlainTalk microphone that comes as part of your computer purchase. This microphone is a convenient way to capture sounds that cannot be recorded directly into the front of the computer. It is also a good way to record your narration several feet away from the iMac, to avoid a slight buzz that is produced from the computer's hard drive.

Use Apple PlainTalk microphone rather than a third-party product, because the ⅛-inch plug extension is longer than other external computer microphones. When plugged into the sound input jack on the side of the computer, this extended plug makes contact with specific connections in the computer to amplify the audio signal for proper recording. Other microphones may not work properly without the use of an extended jack or special adapter.

You will need to choose the External Mic setting from the Sound Monitoring Source menu in the Sound control panel (or from the Control Strip) when using the Apple PlainTalk microphone.

Step Two: Adding Your Own Narration

With the "Flower of Love" project still open, you can proceed to add your own narration to the movie. The first example is dialogue written for a man's voice; the second was developed for a woman to read. You may want to get a friend to speak one of the gender-specific voices for you, but for the purposes of the lesson, it's fine to record these yourself.

Make sure your microphone is connected to the iMac DV computer and a sound level is registered in the Sounds palette.

1 To begin, you will need to delete or mute the previous narration clips called "Narration #2" and "Narration #3." Select these clips, and either reduce their volume with the slider or press the Delete key to remove them from the timeline. (You can easily restore or replace these clips later.)

2 Move the playhead in the audio viewer to the position of 08:14 in the timeline.

▼ **3** Prepare to record by speaking into the microphone and checking the volume levels in the Sounds palette.

Record Levels The levels indicator above the Record Voice button should produce bouncing signals from left to right. A decent middle range (where the signal never reaches the extreme right end of the indicator) will produce an ideal recording volume.

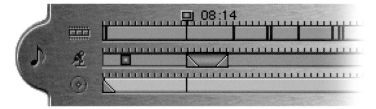

▲ **4** Click the Record Voice button in the Sounds palette, and speak the following lines into the microphone:

"I read the letter one more time, just to make sure I hadn't forgotten anything."

5 Click the Stop button in the Sounds palette to stop the recording when you are finished.

Your voice is recorded onto the narration track in the audio viewer.

6 Next, move the playhead in the audio viewer to the position of 12:17 in the timeline.

▼ **7** Click the Record Voice button in the Sounds palette, and speak the following lines into the microphone:

"Dear John, meet me at the Hotel St. Louis on Monday night. I'll be wearing a rose, the flower of love, on my dress."

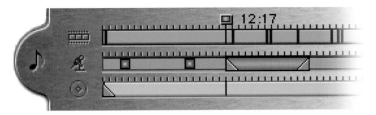

To listen to the narration clips you just recorded, move the playhead to a position just before your voiceovers and press the Space bar.

Once recorded, you can adjust these narration clips in the same way as any other audio file. Set the volume and fade controls to your preference, trying to match the level of the other sound effects for consistency.

If you are not satisfied with the results of your narration, you may remove the clip by pressing the Delete key and try again. In iMovie, you may record your voice as many times as you like. In fact, you may want to try several takes in the same recording and simply edit the best moments from them—the same way you removed extraneous footage from the video clips.

Step Three: Editing Audio Clips in the Timeline

Keep the "Flower of Love" project open, so you can proceed to edit the length of your own narration tracks. The narration clips will appear with crop markers, much like the ones used for trimming video footage.

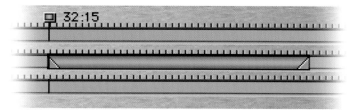

▲ **1** Select any narration clip you wish to edit. A sample is shown above.

▲ **2** At the left end of the narration clip, select the audio crop marker and drag it to the right so it appears within the edges of the clip. You can also position audio crop markers precisely with the arrow keys.

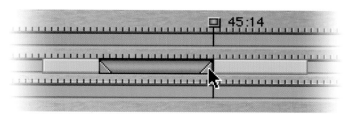

▲ **3** At the right end of the narration clip, drag the audio crop marker to the left and position it within the edges of the clip.

▲ You can leave narration clips exactly like this—with their crop markers set in position. This is handy when you decide to return to the clip and lengthen the duration or reposition the markers.

◀ **4** You can also trim the clip by choosing Crop from the Edit menu. Note that the duration will change as well as the length of the clip in the timeline. Choose the Undo command to restore the clip to its original condition.

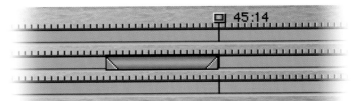

Cropping Audio Once you've cropped an audio clip, the narration will be a shorter clip. You can undo your changes, but once you've saved these clips you can't alter them.

HOW SOUND EFFECTS CAN CHANGE INTENT

Some sound effects can alter the meaning of a sequence. To demonstrate this, a sample of "The Flower of Love" movie was made using several of the preinstalled sound effects included with iMovie. These noises, which include crowds clapping and audience laughter, have been substituted in the clips for comedic effect. Instead of enhancing the Film Noir mood of the sequence, the entrance of a mysterious woman into a man's hotel room is undermined by the sounds of a situation comedy. This example, which can be seen in the "Sitcom Sound.mov" movie in the QuickTime Gallery folder on the DVD-ROM disc, shows how important music and sound effects can be to your movie when establishing the tone of a story. More sound effects are available for free download from the Apple website at **www.apple.com**.

Step Four: Positioning Audio Clips in the Timeline

DVD Keep the "Flower of Love" project open to finish adding narration tracks to the Audio timeline. Because the actors prepared their voiceovers, they have been made available to this lesson as narration clips in the Sounds palette. You can restore the location of the previous clips, "Narration #1–#3," and follow the lesson to complete the movie.

The exact position has been indicated for each clip, but feel free to experiment with the location of the voiceovers for dramatic impact.

▲ **1** With the Sounds palette open, locate the sound effect called "Narration #4" from the list.

2 Drag the voiceover from the list, and position it on the middle track of the Audio timeline.

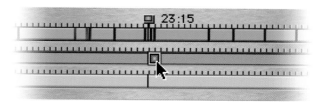

▲ **3** Using your cursor, drag the red square until the playhead indicates the position of 23:15 in the timeline.

Done Your finished project should look like this in the Audio Timeline view. (The exact position of all sound effects is not important.) Make sure your tracks are all activated by clicking the checkboxes at the end of the timeline.

▲ **4** Locate the sound effect called "Narration #5" from the list, drag it into the middle audio track, and position the playhead to indicate 50:29 in the timeline.

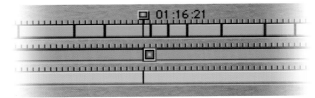

▲ **5** Drag the sound effect called "Narration #6" into the middle audio track, and position it at 01:16:21 in the timeline.

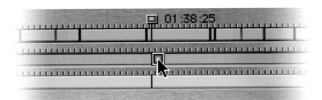

▲ **6** Drag the sound effect called "Narration #7" to the 01:38:25 position in the timeline.

Move the playhead to the beginning of the movie and press the Space bar to play the entire soundtrack. Your timeline should closely resemble the example below.

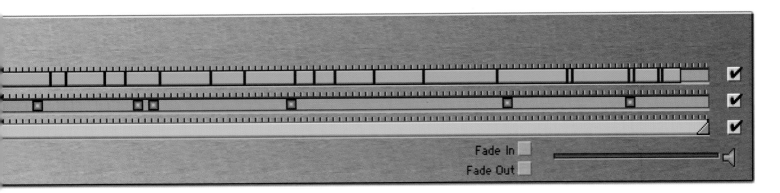

Using the Music Palette

The Music palette in iMovie is a convenient way to bring songs and musical tracks from your own collection of commercial audio CDs directly into your movies. This feature gives you complete control over the recording of individual CD tracks, which can be edited for duration and adjusted for volume and fades, much like narration and video clips.

You can preview songs with the iMovie Music Controller buttons inside the palette. These controls are similar to the ones found in the AppleCD Audio Player, which is part of your system software under the Apple menu. There's even an eject button to let you change which CD is in your iMac computer. You can also eject CDs by dragging the disc icon on the Desktop to the Trash.

Step Five: Adding Music from an Audio CD

Due to the limitations of the DVD-ROM disc, this lesson requires you to insert your own audio CD into your iMac computer. You may want to delete the musical score at the bottom track of the Audio timeline before creating a new music clip.

1 Click the Music button to open the Music palette.

2 Once an audio CD has been inserted into your CD-ROM drive, its playlist will appear in the palette.

3 If music begins to play immediately, click the Stop button. Note that all of the buttons in the Music palette are similar to the video controls in the Monitor window.

4 Select any track from the list in the Music palette by clicking its name. You can double-click or press the Play button to listen to the track. Once you've found a track you like, click the Stop button.

To adjust the volume level, drag the thumbwheel in the Monitor.

5 Position the playhead on the bottom track of the Audio timeline to the beginning of your movie (or press your keyboard's Home key).

6 With your favorite track still highlighted, click the Record Music button in the Music palette. An audio clip will appear in the bottom track and extend as the music plays.

You can click the Stop button at any time. However, the clip will stop automatically at the end of the track.

Press the Home key on your keyboard and listen to the movie with a new musical score.

Importing Other Audio Files

Another way to bring audio files into iMovie is to use the Import feature. Much like the picture import capabilities of iMovie, the audio import function is limited. You can only convert audio in the Audio Interchange File Format (AIFF). An AIFF file is a popular digital audio file that can be used by many sound applications. AIFF is a common file type that is often exchanged over the Internet.

You can import AIFF files by selecting Import File from the File menu. AIFF files imported into iMovie will appear on the bottom track of the timeline. You can move the playhead in the Audio viewer to pinpoint the insertion point before importing the audio file. The AIFF clip includes markers so that it can be cropped just like a narration or music clip.

Importing Audio iMovie accepts sound files imported in the AIFF format, a common file type exchanged among sound professionals and audiophiles over the Internet.

ADDITIONAL AUDIO CLIPS
SEVERAL ADDITIONAL SOUND EFFECTS ARE INCLUDED FOR YOUR USE IN THE FREEBIES FOLDER ON THE DVD-ROM. YOU CAN GET FREE SOUND RESOURCES BY VISITING THE IMOVIE SECTION OF APPLE'S WEB SITE OR THE MAKING IMOVIES WEB PAGE AT www.makingimovies.com.

Other Ways of Importing Audio Files

There are a few alternatives to importing audio files of different formats. An upgrade of your QuickTime Player software will let you translate various audio samples (such as MP3 and WAV files) into the AIFF format. To get the upgrade, you must visit Apple's Web site, fill out an online registration form, and purchase QuickTime Pro, a version of the player software that offers useful multimedia authoring features. These include the ability to extract audio from video footage, convert graphics into other formats, and save video clips as DV files for import into iMovie.

If you would like to make any sound effect a permanent part of your Sounds palette, you can add its file to the Resources folder in your iMovie application. (Removing sounds from that folder will remove them from the Sounds palette.) To do this, locate the iMovie folder on your hard drive. Inside you will find a Resources folder that contains a Sound Effects folder. This is where the audio clips that appear on the list in the Sounds palette are stored. If you drag any AIFF audio file into this folder before launching the iMovie application, The additions will appear in the Sounds palette when you launch iMovie.

Converting Audio to AIFF Upgrading to QuickTime Pro will allow you to convert a handful of popular audio file types, such as MP3 and WAV, to the AIFF format.

Adding Sound Effects You can make your own sound effects a permanent part of the iMovie Sounds Palette by placing AIFF files inside the Sound Effects folder on your hard drive, located within the Resources folder where your iMovie application resides.

chapter six

adding titles and transition effects

With a little imagination and some simple effects, you can dramatically enhance your stories. Fortunately, iMovie includes a selection of commonly used effects to make your stories flow smoothly from scene to scene. These special effects make movies look more professional and can save you considerable time when adding a finished look to your movie. In this chapter, we will enhance our movies with some special effects, particularly Titles and Transitions. We'll cover these features together because they share similar interface concepts and, when used together, they clearly illustrate how the use of effects can drastically alter the style and tempo (and in many cases, the meaning) of your final project.

Special effects make movies look more professional.

Use Effects Sparingly

Believe it or not, special effects won't improve your story; they will only enhance it. So if your work isn't compelling without the use of effects, it's not likely to improve once you add titles or transitions. Some moviemakers overdo it; it is the mark of an amateur to add too many titles and transitions. Try to use a bare minimum of effects in your movie. If you can't think of a good reason to use an effect, it probably isn't critical to the telling of your story.

Titles for Movies

In a movie theater, titles are often the first thing you see, and they can immediately establish the mood of a story. If you are a frequent moviegoer, you'll recognize the titles of a Woody Allen film, a straightforward set of text displayed against a black background. The lavish costume dramas of Merchant-Ivory films often include colorful fonts that allude to the fancy dress of the period. Titles can be more than just text; they can include special effects that, when combined with text, hint at the drama of the story to come. Perhaps you recall the prelude to *Star Wars,* with its opening titles drifting out into the infinite reaches of space and simultaneously introducing the first chapter of an ongoing saga.

How Titles Work in iMovie

With iMovie, you can add easily create professional-looking titles using a variety of customizable effects, letting you decide which font, color, or animation style is best for your movie. These title effects are "rendered" over your video footage by superimposing the text onto any images in the background. iMovie can render the title effects over your video clip, still pictures, or a solid black background. These rendered effects are presented to you on-screen in a "nondestructive" preview image, which means the text is never directly applied to the captured DV footage until you are ready to export your final movie. This way, you can change your mind at any time and edit or delete titles from your movie while retaining the original quality of your video images.

The Titles Palette

To activate the Titles palette, click the Titles button in the Effects menu. All of the features and functions you'll need to create title effects are included on this palette. These settings are not accessible from anywhere else in iMovie.

Choosing a Title Effect

iMovie includes an excellent selection of built-in title effects that you can drag and drop directly into the project timeline. While many of these settings can be customized, the predefined animations will save you considerable time and give your movie some outstanding and professional results. By choosing an animation style in the scrolling list of title effects, you can instantly see a thumbnail preview of a sample title in that style appearing over a clip of video. The footage used in the thumbnail is determined by the position of the playhead in the Clip Viewer. To preview a title effect over a different video clip, simply position the playhead in front of the clip in the timeline or highlight the footage in the Clip Viewer.

Setting the Duration of an Effect

You can adjust the time it takes to execute a title effect by using the slider at the top of the Titles palette. The shorter the duration, the faster the effect will appear and disappear. For cumbersome titles, vital pieces of information, or an extensive list of credits, it is best to set the duration for longer lengths, giving your audience a chance to read everything before the titles fade away.

The numerical value of the title effect duration appears in the bottom right corner of the thumbnail window. The length of the effect is expressed in seconds followed by frames. iMovie renders effects to the video clips in increments of 30 frames per second. For instance, an effect that is one frame short of 4 seconds will be displayed in the thumbnail window as 03:29. An effect that should last half a second should be set with the slider at 00:15 (or 15 frames).

The duration of a title is largely dependent on the clip it uses as a background; no effect can be set for a longer duration than the clip it is superimposed over.

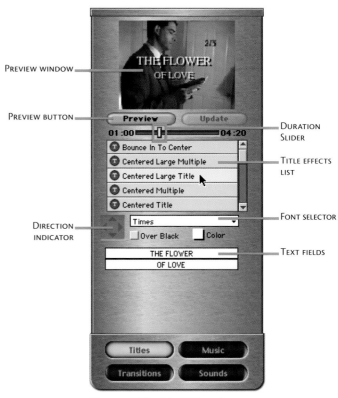

Custom Titles The Titles palette helps you create custom titles in a variety of styles. Its controls include settings for font color, effect duration, and the direction of the animation.

Setting the Direction of the Animation

The small arrows in the center of the Titles palette determine the direction in which your titles will animate. Some of the built-in effects do not offer this feature, and others are only slightly affected by changes in direction. You can experiment with the settings and preview the changes immediately in the thumbnail window.

Selecting a Font for Your Titles

You can instantly change the font (or typeface) of your titles within iMovie by using the pull-down list in the center of the Titles palette. The list that appears in this menu reflects all of the TrueType or PostScript fonts currently available in your System Folder.

The font you select for your movie titles will instantly lend a mood or personality to your story, so it's important to choose carefully. An elegant, scripted typeface may be ideal for a wedding or formal event, but using a more garish or modern font for the same footage might evoke a comical reaction from your audience. If your story has a science-fiction or high-tech theme, you could try contemporary fonts that seem computer-generated. Generally, you'll want to pick one font and stay with it throughout your movie. Although iMovie will allow you to use different fonts for each title you create, this practice may confuse your viewers, suggesting that the plot or location has suddenly changed. Consistency and clarity should dictate your typeface choices.

Legibility is also a concern. As a rule, it is better to use serif typefaces for title effects that have long sentences, multiple names, or words that require both uppercase and lowercase letterforms. Sans serif typefaces are ideal for short, bold headlines as well as for numbers or symbols.

Choosing the Color of Your Titles

Titles can be further customized through a selection of 16 colors. To access one of these color options, click the square swatch next to the word Color in the palette. Holding your mouse button down, drag your cursor to the desired color before letting go. Your color selection will appear as the default color until the next time you change it.

For experienced Macintosh users, the color choices may seem terribly limited. There is a good reason for this, however. Many of the bright custom colors you might commonly pick in computer applications would not appear correctly on a standard television set. While they might look vibrant and consistent on a computer monitor, many colors will pulsate or shift in hue when shown on TV. The iMovie color palette has been restricted to 16 colors that adhere to the National Television Standards Committee (NTSC) guidelines for broadcasting. These colors will help your movie retain a professional look that is consistent with the quality of digital video.

TITLES FOR WEB MOVIES

When choosing a title effect, you should think about where your movie will likely be seen. If you intend to show it to family and friends on a television set, then nearly all of the title effects included with iMovie will work superbly. However, if you wish to stream your movies over the Internet, you will want to avoid title effects that display text in small sizes, such as the Music Video or Stripe Subtitle options. When shown on a computer monitor at 320x240 pixels, these words will be illegible. Also, animated effects such as the Rolling Credits or Scrolling Block will ultimately compress better if they are displayed against a still image or a black background rather than over moving video. Also, effects that animate one letter at a time, such as the Flying Letters or Typewriter options, will put greater demands on the compression software. This ultimately translates to lengthier download times for your audience of online moviegoers.

It is a good idea to preview clips before choosing colors for your titles. You will want to pick colors that will sharply contrast with the footage when titles are superimposed over the clip. Dark scenes will require light colors; daylight will need dark type. Use neutral tones when the luminance of your footage changes rapidly within the same scene. To further distinguish your titles from their background, iMovie automatically places a drop shadow beneath all titles that appear over moving video footage or still images.

Switch Views To manipulate title effects more easily, switch your timeline to the Clip Viewer.

Previewing Your Effect

The Titles palette contains a small thumbnail window to give you a quick visual sense of the title effect options. As you choose the different settings, the thumbnail window displays the changes immediately. However, if you prefer to see changes as they will appear in the final rendered effect, click the Preview button at any time and a larger display will appear in the Clip Monitor. As you change the settings, you will need to click the Preview button to see any updates in the Clip Monitor.

WHY ONLY 16 COLORS?

DESPITE A NUMBER OF OF CUSTOMIZABLE OPTIONS IN THE TITLES PALETTE, THERE ARE ONLY 16 COLORS AVAILABLE FOR TEXT. THESE CHOICES REPRESENT A RANGE OF COLORS THAT ARE "BROADCAST-SAFE," A TERM WHICH REFERS TO COLORS THAT CAN BE FAITHFULLY REPRODUCED ON A STANDARD NTSC TELEVISION SET.

Lesson: Adding Titles to Movies

Adding opening and closing credits to a movie are just some of the things you can do with the title effects in iMovie. Combined with using still images or video footage, you can create moving text that adds life to scenes and supplies important information. Many of the predefined settings were designed to look like common effects seen in music videos, news broadcasts, and major blockbuster movies. The following steps use several of these effects to turn the previous lesson files into a silent movie, complete with old-fashioned title cards.

Step One: Creating Titles over a Black Background

To demonstrate the key principles in this lesson, the "Adding Titles" project uses footage from the last lesson. Several of the video clips will appear in the Clip Shelf, but they are not necessary to complete the lesson. The audio and sound-effect tracks have been disabled to create the illusion of a silent movie. (A sample of the finished movie, "Silent Flower.mov," can be found in the QuickTime Gallery folder on the DVD-ROM disc.) Begin by adding a simple opening title over a black background, using one of the predefined title effects.

1 Choose Open Project from the File Menu. Locate the "Adding Titles" Folder, and select the "Silent Flower" project.

2 With the "Silent Flower" project now open, position the Playhead at the start of the timeline (or simply highlight the first icon in the Clip Viewer).

3 Click the Title button in the Effects menu to reveal the palette options. Scroll down the style list in the Titles palette, and choose Flying Words from the list.

4 Set the effect duration to 01:12 by adjusting the slider control at the top of the palette.

5 Click the font pull-down menu, and choose Times from the list of available fonts.

6 Be sure the box labeled Over Black is checked. This will superimpose your title over a black background and prevent iMovie from placing the text over any video clips.

7 Click the Color swatch, and pick a color for your text from the pop-up palette. White will work best for this title.

8 Choose from which direction you want the words to "fly" into the frame.

9 Highlight the phrase in the upper text field. Type your name in this space, replacing the previous phrase.

10 Highlight the phrase in the lower text field. Type the word "Presents" in its place.

You can click the Preview button at the top of the titles palette to see a preview of the effect in the Clip Monitor.

11 Once these settings are satisfactory, drag the Flying Words title from the style list and place it in front of the first clip in the clip viewer.

Notice the small red status bar that appears at the base of the new clip. This is an indicator that the title effect is being rendered. A counter will also display the number of total frames rendered when you have the Clip Viewer selected.

When the render status is complete, press the Home key on your keyboard and then the Space bar to play your movie with its new title.

12 Quickly add one more title over a black background. Scroll through the style list in the Titles palette, and choose Bounce In To Center from the list. Be sure the box labeled Over Black is checked.

13 Highlight the text in the upper field, and replace the phrase with the word "THE." Highlight the text in the lower field, and type the word "END" in its place.

14 Drag the Bounce In To Center title from the style list, and place it behind the last clip in the timeline.

Deleting the Effect

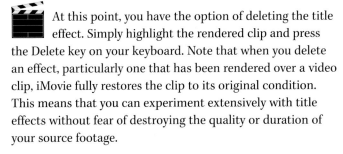 At this point, you have the option of deleting the title effect. Simply highlight the rendered clip and press the Delete key on your keyboard. Note that when you delete an effect, particularly one that has been rendered over a video clip, iMovie fully restores the clip to its original condition. This means that you can experiment extensively with title effects without fear of destroying the quality or duration of your source footage.

You may also elect to delete the clip with the remaining frames. However, this action is irreversible after you have saved your project and quit the iMovie application. If you intend to use this excess footage later, you may drag the clip to the shelf for future use.

> **PUTTING A HALT TO RENDERING** YOU CAN STOP iMOVIE FROM CREAT-ING OR UPDATING AN EFFECT, EVEN WHILE IT IS STILL RENDERING. USE THE UNDO OPTION IN THE EDIT MENU, OR TYPE COMMAND-Z ON YOUR KEYBOARD, TO INTERRUPT THE PROCESS. YOUR CLIP WILL IMMEDI-ATELY REVERT TO ITS LAST SETTINGS.

Rendering Effects

 Unlike other video applications, iMovie does not require you to wait for rendering to be completed before allowing you to keep working. This process of rendering is essentially "invisible" to the moviemaker, who can continue to create new effects while iMovie diligently works in the background, compositing elements together and superimposing text and transitions over the video clips.

Despite this invisible rendering feature, you may at times wish to intervene and stop a long render before it is completed. By choosing the Undo option in the Edit Menu, or typing the keyboard shortcut Command-Z, you can put a halt to long rendering processes. Your clips will return to their previous condition, unaffected by the interruption. Unfortunately, any changes in the Title Palette, such as corrections to the spelling of a name, will be lost when reverting to the prior settings.

TIP

ADDING (AND DELETING) MULTIPLE TITLES
SEVERAL OF THE TITLE EFFECTS IN iMOVIE ALLOW YOU TO INCLUDE MULTIPLE TEXT FILES FOR SCROLLING CREDITS OR SEPARATING PHRASES. THE PAUSE BETWEEN MULTIPLE TITLE EFFECTS, AS WELL AS THE PACE AT WHICH THEY SCROLL, IS DETERMINED BY THE OVERALL DURATION SET BY THE EFFECT SLIDER. YOU CAN GENERATE MORE TEXT FIELDS BY CLICKING THE "ADD" BUTTON. TO ELIMINATE A TEXT FIELD, SIMPLY SELECT ITS BORDER AND DRAG IT TO THE TRASH.

Step Two: Creating Titles over Video

Now that you've added opening titles over a black background, you're ready to create some titles over moving video footage to provide more dynamic titles for your movie.

1 In the Titles palette, choose Centered Large Title from the style list. Adjust the duration slider to 02:00.

2 Choose Times from the font pull-down menu. Click the Color picker, and choose white for your credit text.

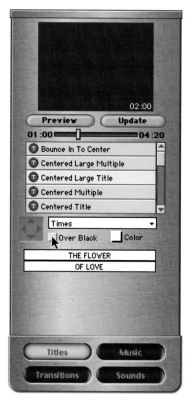

▲ **3** Make sure the box labeled Over Black is unchecked. This will superimpose your title over the video footage of the first clip.

4 Highlight the phrases in the text fields and replace them with the phrase "The Flower" and "Of Love" in the upper and lower text fields respectively.

◀ **5** Click the Preview button to display the results of the effect in the thumbnail window.

▲ **6** Now, drag the Centered Large Title style and place it to the left of the clip labeled "Appears At Door." A red status bar will appear at the bottom of the clip to indicate that iMovie is rendering the effect.

Applying this title effect to the timeline will automatically produce two separate clips: a new 02:00 clip with the title superimposed over a portion of the original clip and another clip with the remaining frames. Move the playhead to the beginning of the movie, and preview your effect.

Updating an Effect

 At any time during the creation of your movie, you can easily change the settings of your title effects. Simply highlight the title clip in the timeline and double-click it. The Titles palette will immediately pop up to display the current settings of your effect. Now, you can correct the spelling of a name in your title, extend or shorten its duration, choose a different font, select another color, or alter the style and direction of the animation. To preview your changes, click the Preview button. When you are satisfied, click the Update button. Despite the presence of a title clip in the timeline, your edits will replace the existing settings without creating a new title. The red status bar at the base of the clip will indicate that the new effects are being rendered.

Of course, the speed and ease of the Titles palette makes it tempting to simply delete a title clip from the timeline and start again from scratch. But in many ways, updating a clip is better than creating a new one. First, this feature allows you to make changes to a title without upsetting the order of clips in the timeline. Likewise, it's a great way to preview potential changes before committing them to your title clips. The Update button is also extremely efficient when you are making a series of small changes to titles that have been duplicated from a single clip.

Step Three: Creating Titles over a Still Image

To create the look of silent movie title cards, you can easily add dialogue between your clips by using some title effects over still images. For this lesson, a graphic file has been inserted into the timeline to provide a decorative background for this effect. You can export your own background images in PICT, GIF, or JPEG format from any paint program and import them into iMovie.

▲ **1** Select the still image clip called "Title Card #1" in the Clip Viewer. Note: The field at the top of the timeline will reflect the clip duration of 02:00 seconds.

2 In the Titles palette, make sure Centered Large Title is still the selected style from the list, Times is the font, and the box labeled Over Black is unchecked. The Color picker should still display white for your text.

▶ **3** Move the duration slider to 01:29.

Some title effects must have a shorter duration than the clip they are intended to superimpose. By setting the slider to 01:29, the title will superimpose much of the still image clip without exceeding the limits of the application.

4 Highlight the phrases in the text fields and replace them with the phrase "Excuse me," and "are you John?" in the upper and lower text fields respectively.

5 Then, drag the Centered Large Titles style and place it to the left of the clip labeled "Title Card #1." A red status bar will appear at the bottom of the clip and the name will display as "Excuse Me," when rendering is complete.

6 Next, select the still image clip called "Title Card #2" in the Clip Viewer. Leave the Centered Large Title selected as the style from the list in the Titles palette.

7 Highlight the phrases in the text fields and replace them with the phrase "Is it really" and "YOU?" in the upper and lower text fields respectively.

8 Then, drag the Centered Large Title style and place it to the left of the clip labeled "Title Card #2." A red status bar will appear at the bottom of the clip and the name will display as "Is it really" when rendering is complete.

Duplicating a Title Effect

 A great virtue of iMovie is its ability to automate repetitive tasks, specifically in the area of duplicating clips. This comes in handy if you wish to reuse a piece of footage throughout your movie. Even though you have imported the scene from your DV camcorder just once, you can create multiple clips from that single source. Simply select any clip on the Shelf or in the project timeline and choose the Copy and Paste functions of the Edit menu to duplicate them. iMovie won't take up precious storage space by creating additional versions on your hard disk. Instead, it keeps track of these duplicated clips in the timeline as sort of "virtual icons" and calls upon the original source file only when exporting your final movie to tape.

Fortunately, because title effects are also represented in the timeline as clips (much like captured footage), they are easy to duplicate. This can really streamline projects with lots of title effects. This also means that title effects can be dragged from the timeline into the Clip Shelf if you need to reorder your scenes.

IMPORTING GRAPHICS AS TITLE BACKGROUNDS
WHEN YOU IMPORT A PICT, GIF, OR JPEG STILL IMAGE, IT WILL AUTOMATICALLY APPEAR AS A CLIP WITH A DEFAULT DURATION OF 10 SECONDS. YOU CAN EDIT THIS DURATION BUT ONLY WHEN THE IMAGE IS PRESENT IN THE CLIP VIEWER. ONCE SELECTED, THE NAME AND DURATION WILL APPEAR AT THE TOP OF THE TIMELINE. THEN, SIMPLY HIGHLIGHT THE DURATION AND TYPE IN A NEW VALUE.

Step Four: Duplicating and Updating Title Effects

If you must create several title effects with similar attributes, it may be useful to use the Copy and Paste functions of the iMovie software to expedite your task. You can also use the Update button in the Titles palette to edit individual effects without altering their settings.

▲ **1** Locate the previously rendered clip called "Is it really," and highlight the icon in the timeline. Duplicate the clip by first choosing Copy function in the Edit menu and then returning to the Edit menu and selecting Paste. A duplicate clip will appear in the timeline.

▶ **2** Drag the duplicate clip and place it between the "She Smiles" and "He Speaks" clips in the project timeline.

3 Double-click the duplicate clip to activate the current effect settings in the Titles palette. All of the settings in the duplicate clip will appear exactly as they are in the original Title clip.

4 Replace the dialogue in the text fields with the phrases "You're exactly" and "like I imagined."

5 Click the Update button at the top of the Titles palette to render the effect. A red status bar will indicate that the titles are rendering.

6 Duplicate another Title clip by choosing the Paste function in the Edit menu. A duplicate will appear in the timeline. Drag it into position in the timeline between the "She Smiles" and "Hears Knock" clips.

7 Double-click the duplicate clip to activate the current effect settings in the Titles palette. Highlight the phrases in the text fields. and replace them with "Is your name" and "John Washington?"

8 Paste another duplicate clip into the timeline, and drag it to the position in the timeline between the "No, Robertson" and "She Bolts" clips.

9 Double-click the duplicate clip to activate the current effect settings. Highlight the phrases in the text fields, and replace them with "No, my name is" and "John Robertson!"

10 Click the Update button, and wait for the render to finish before seeing the results.

When all effects have been rendered, press the Home key on your keyboard and then the Space bar to play your finished movie with all of the title effects.

How Transitions Work in iMovie

The selection of transition effects included with iMovie are rather sophisticated; they are comparable to effects used in professional video editing systems for decades. They can give your movies remarkable authority when used skillfully. Consider each transition effect carefully before applied, for each brings with it the power to alter the meaning of your sequences. Often these effects add important emphasis, but they can also ruin the flow of action between clips.

Unlike title effects, transitions are not "superimposed" over your video footage. They are the result of combining two video signals into a new clip, containing new frames created from the complex calculations performed during rendering. iMovie presents these Transition effects as "nondestructive" footage, which means your original source clips are never directly affected by the transition process.

The Transitions Palette

The built-in palette of transition effects is activated once you click the Transitions button in the Effects menu. Transition settings are only accessible from this palette and can be applied to any of the video or still image clips in the timeline. Transitions cannot be applied to other transition effects or to audio tracks, although the synchronized audio of your video clips may be altered during the application of transition effects.

Choosing a Transition Effect

Selecting a predefined effect in the Transitions palette is straightforward. Scroll through the list of available effects and double-click any selection to see a preview in the display window. The settings in the Transitions palette include all of the functions needed to control the style, duration, and direction of the effect.

Similarities Between Titles and Transitions

Much like the Title effects, transitions can be dropped directly into the timeline from the Effects menu palette. Many of the controls—including the duration slider, the direction tool, and the display buttons—work exactly as they do in the Titles palette. Likewise, when transitions are dragged into the project timeline, the existing clips will move to indicate the space the effect will occupy when dropped. Once applied, transitions will display a red status bar during rendering. As with titles, you can delete, restore, and update them using the controls demonstrated in the previous lesson.

Differences Between Titles and Transitions

Transitions do not appear in the timeline as typical video clips; they have a smaller, rectangular shape to distinguish them from the other elements in the Clip Viewer. Unlike title effects, transitions cannot be duplicated using the copy and paste functions. (However, you can use some palette settings to quickly repeat certain effects.)

Lesson: Adding Transitions to Movies

Transitions in iMovie are as easy as dragging and dropping, but their impact on your video footage can be much more complex. In this lesson, we've edited and assembled the movie footage without the use of transitions. The result is a movie with simple cuts and no frills. However, you will see how transition effects add a touch of grace and professional polish to these shots and create a visual tapestry that reinforces the suspense in the story.

Step One: Placing Transitions in the Timeline

This lesson features new movie footage from the "General Hysteria" project, located on the DVD-ROM disc. Although the soundtrack may seem slightly out of sync at first viewing, you will shorten the duration of the video footage by adding transition effects throughout the lesson. A sample of the finished movie, "General Hysteria.mov," can be found in the QuickTime Gallery folder on the disc. Begin by closing your previous project and opening the Adding Transitions folder.

1 Choose Open Project from the File Menu. Locate the "Adding Transitions" Folder, and select the "General Hysteria" project.

2 With the "General Hysteria" project now open, position the playhead at the start of the timeline (or simply highlight the first icon in the Clip Viewer). Play the movie to see how it looks with no transitions.

3 Click the Transition button in the Effects menu to reveal the palette options. Scroll down the style list in the Transitions palette, and choose Fade In from the list.

4 Set the effect duration to 01:02 by adjusting the slider control at the top of the palette.

To preview the effect, make sure you have selected the first clip in the project timeline. Once the clip is highlighted, you can press the Preview button in the Transitions palette to see the effect displayed at the top of the palette.

5 Drag the Fade In transition from the style list, and place it in front of the first clip in the timeline.

6 To see the Fade In transition in the Preview, select the triangular effect icon in the timeline, hold down the Shift key, and select the Opening Shot clip. Both clips will become highlighted and both will appear in the Monitor window. Press the Space bar to play the clips together.

7 Repeat this effect using the Fade Out style (with the same duration) and dragging the transition to the end of the timeline, placing it behind the last clip.

8 Next, scroll through the style list in the Transitions palette and choose Cross Dissolve.

◀ **9** Set the effect duration to 00:22 by adjusting the slider control at the top of the palette.

◀ **10** Drag the Cross Dissolve transition into the timeline, and place it in front of the clip called "First March." Immediately, the red status bar will indicate that the clip is rendering.

◀ **11** Repeat the Cross Dissolve style for the next effect. Set the duration to 02:00.

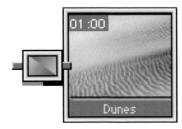

◀ **12** Drag and drop the transition into the timeline just in front of the clip called "Dunes."

13 Repeat the Cross Dissolve style once more, this time setting the duration to 02:04.

14 Place the transition in the timeline to the left of the clip called "Stop For Drink."

15 And finally, choose the Cross Dissolve Slow style, and set the duration to 02:12 by adjusting the slider.

16 Place this transition to the left of the clip called "Hands Up" in the project timeline.

After all effects have been rendered, press the Home key on your keyboard and then the Space bar to play the movie with these transition effects. Notice how the cross dissolve effects suggest a greater passage of time than the sequence without any transitions.

Step Two: Processing Multiple Transitions

Keep this lesson open, as the following steps outline ways of using the Transition palette to maximize your productivity when applying numerous effects.

1 With the "General Hysteria" project still open, select the rectangular Cross Dissolve effect icon just before the "Stop For Drink" clip. Make sure the effect is highlighted by double-clicking it.

◀ **2** The Transitions palette will display the settings from the effect, with the duration set at 02:04.

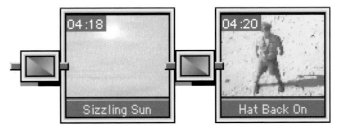

▲ **3** Now, apply two identical effects with these exact settings by quickly dragging the transition into the timeline in rapid succession, once in front of the "Sizzling Sun" clip and then again in front of the "Hat Back On" clip.

You will see both icons appear with red status bars, indicating that both are rendering simultaneously. iMovie can process multiple clips at once while you continue to work on other parts of your movie.

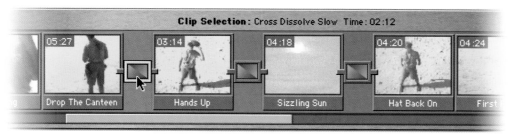

▲ **4** Repeat this technique by selecting the Cross Dissolve Slow effect just before the "Hands Up" clip. Double-click the rectangular icon to activate the effect's previous settings in the Transitions palette.

◄ **5** Change the duration setting to 02:28 by adjusting the slider.

▲ **6** Now, quickly drag two identical effects with these exact settings into the timeline in rapid succession, once in front of the "First Fall" clip and then again in front of the "Swaying Head" clip.

Press the Home key on your keyboard and then the Space bar to play the movie with these transition effects.

Step Three: Updating Transitions in the Timeline

Continuing with the "General Hysteria" lesson, you can explore the Update button in the Transitions palette to further automate the application of similar effects.

1 Keep the "General Hysteria" project open, and scroll down the style list in the Transitions palette until you locate the Overlap effect from the list.

◀ **2** Set the duration to 01:00. Then, click the "Drops Gear Belt" clip in the timeline before pressing the Preview button in the palette window.

The Overlap effect is slightly different than the Cross Dissolve effect: It freezes the last frame of the previous clip and blends the incoming frames without using equal amounts of footage from both clips.

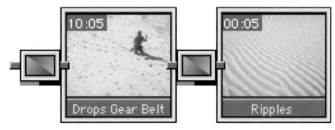

▲ **3** As with the previous example, drag two effects into the timeline in succession, placing one in front of the "Drops Gear Belt" clip and the other in front of the "Ripples" clip.

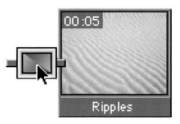

◀ **4** Once the effects have rendered, select the second effect in the timeline, the one before the "Ripples" clip. Double-click the effect icon to ensure that the effect settings are activated.

◄ **5** In the Transitions palette, scroll through the styles and choose Cross Dissolve from the list. Then, press the Update button.

◄ **6** Next, drag two of the same Cross Dissolve effects into the timeline in succession, placing one in front of the "Looks At Sun" clip and the other in front of the "Sunspot" icon.

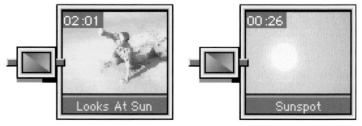

▲ **7** Now, select those same effect icons individually in the timeline, change their durations to 02:04, and press the Update button. There is no need to wait for the render status to finish before applying another Update to an effect.

Step Four: Using Transitions Creatively

Cross dissolves are popular transition effects because they are subtle. In this movie, they create a great sense of timelessness and distance. However, other effects can be just as effective for their sudden explosion on the screen or their extreme visual impact.

1 With the "General Hysteria" project still open, scroll down the style list in the Transitions palette until you locate the Wash Out effect from the list.

◀ **2** After setting the duration slider to 01:06, drag the transition into the timeline and place it in front of the clip called "Looking At Birds."

Wash in; Wash out Some transitions are designed to work well together to create dynamic visual effects. In this case, the Wash Out effect from the previous clip suggests that the intense heat from the sun is blinding the soldier.

▲ **3** Repeat this step using the same duration, but choose the Wash In effect from the style list. This time, place the transition just after the last effect icon (this will fall between the effect icon and the "Looking At Birds" clip).

Symmetrical Shots Although dissolves are common transitions in many situations, they are best used to express the symmetry between shots. Here, the widening mouth of the screaming man dissolves into the ever-present sphere in the sky. A long, slow transition helps punctuate the similarities of these compositions.

4 Next, scroll down the style list in the Transitions palette until you locate the Cross Dissolve Slow effect from the list.

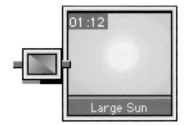

5 After setting the duration slider to 02:28, drag the Cross Dissolve Slow transition into the timeline and place it in front of the clip called "Large Sun."

6 At last, scroll down the style list in the Transitions palette until you locate the Warp Out effect from the list. Then, set the duration slider to 00:12

Warp Out To jolt the audience from the dream sequence, it is best to use an unorthodox transition of very short duration (less than 15 frames). The Warp Out effect literally breaks the image at the center and peels it away to reveal the underlying footage.

7 Drag the Warp Out transition into the timeline, and place it in front of the clip called "Awakening."

Once you have finished, press the Home key on your keyboard and then the Space bar to play the movie with these transition effects.

Adjusting to Changes in the Timeline

 Many transitions and titles will alter the overall duration: An imported graphic will extend the movie's final length, and the blending of frames required to execute a cross dissolve will ultimately shorten the time of individual tracks. This can be a source of frustration if the music, narration, and sound-effects clips that have been previously set are no longer synchronized. Thankfully, it is relatively painless to correct this problem. Simply return to Audio timeline view and drag the affected clips to any location within the project timeline.

We presented the audio lessons before the effects lessons because it is generally better to create your titles and transitions with the soundtracks as an initial reference. It is often desirable to align your effects with the tempo and highlights of the score. Traditionally, audio is the last thing filmmakers concern themselves with, due to the expense and inconvenience of adapting audio to a working print. But in iMovie, it's easy to make changes to the soundtrack, so you are free to experiment with audio as early in the process as you'd like. Then, you can modify the original score to correct mistakes caused by the introduction of titles and transitions.

chapter seven

saving your movie

Once your masterpiece is finished, you have many options

to help give your movie the longest life possible. Because

DV footage takes up a lot of hard disk space, you won't want

to store it on your drive for too long. Fortunately, iMovie

provides several output formats in which to save the final

DV footage elsewhere.

This chapter looks

at procedures for

transferring the enhanced movie

footage—complete with sound, title,

and transition effects—out of the iMac

computer. You may wish to premiere your movie on the

television set for the whole family or create copies of the

video on other tape formats such as VHS to show to friends.

This chapter talks about issues of archiving, compression,

and playback.

Give your movie the longest life possible.

Saving Your Project Files

Before exporting your movie to a file format suitable for Web distribution, you will want to save the iMovie project files. That way, system errors or unforeseen power interruptions won't cause you to lose your edits or effects.

Exporting Your Finished Movie

Storing your files on the hard disk is not viable long-term since you'll want to clear the disk space for other projects. How to store your movie project? The most economical way is to export your finished movie to a DV tape through the FireWire connection to your camcorder.

So far, no other method matches the mini-DV format for speed, capacity, and affordability. Mini-DV tapes are durable, compact, and inexpensive, making them ideal for archiving your footage. Tapes aren't impervious to damage, so keep them in a protective case and avoid exposing them to extreme changes in temperature.

You can further protect your archived footage by switching the small tab on the tape cartridge to the protected position. Locking tapes is a good idea; it can prevent others from accidentally recording over your footage. Check the instructions that come with your tapes for more tips on long-term care.

TAPE CARE
IF YOU INTEND TO ARCHIVE FOOTAGE ON A DV VIDEOTAPE FOR LONG STRETCHES OF TIME, MAKE SURE YOU TAKE IT OUT OF STORAGE SEMIANNUALLY, FAST-FORWARD THE TAPE TO THE END OF ITS REEL, AND REWIND IT TO ENSURE THAT IT STAYS IN PROPER WORKING CONDITION.

Save Before Export Always save your projects before exporting. During longer compressions, as the iMovie software squeezes your movie into a QuickTime file, a system error or power outtage could jeopardize hours of hard work.

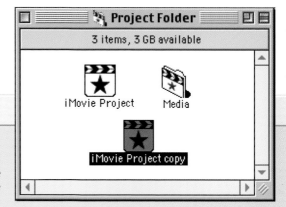

DUPLICATING PROJECT FOLDERS

You may occasionally want to include the same clip in several movies. A great trick for reusing iMovie files without recapturing redundant clips is to duplicate your projects, leaving the Media folder as a shared source of footage. This procedure is useful if you'd like to experiment with alternative movie ideas, but keep the original project settings in another file. First, locate your iMovie project folder on the hard drive and open it to reveal the project file and the Media folder. Highlight just the project file icon by clicking it. Do not highlight the Media folder. Once the icon is selected, choose Duplicate from the Finder's File menu. (If you don't see the Duplicate command, you've probably launched the iMovie application and must quit to return to the Finder.) Once you have duplicated the project file, a new icon will appear on the hard disk next to the original file. Rename this icon by clicking it and pressing the Return key. Be careful to keep this file in the same folder as the original project file and its corresponding Media folder. When you double-click the new icon, the duplicate file will launch iMovie. The new name will be displayed in the Timeline window, and the clips will be exactly the same as the footage used in the original project.

Exporting to Mini-DV Tapes

When you are ready to transfer your footage to tape, select the Export Movie command from iMovie's File menu. A dialog box will appear, prompting you to prepare your camcorder for recording. If the camcorder is not connected to the iMac computer by a FireWire cable, a warning will pop up. You will also receive warnings if the camera is not operating due to a lack of power or the absence of a tape.

Usually, iMovie will wait a moment before your camera is ready, allowing time for the camera's tape heads to rewind and position themselves for recording. In most camcorders, this takes only a few seconds. You also have the option of providing a "leader" to your exported footage, a few seconds of blackness that prepares the viewer for the coming movie. This black leader is ideal when making copies of your footage to a VHS tape or another VCR, because it eases the transition from your television's white noise to the beginning of the movie.

Making a Copy on a VHS Tape

Once you've successfully transferred your movie to a digital videotape, you can use the audio/video cables supplied with your DV camcorder to watch your movie on a standard television set.

You can also use these cables to connect the camcorder to your VCR and copy your movie to a VHS tape for distribution to friends and family. For complete guidelines on copying from the DV tapes to VHS, consult the manufacturer's instructions included with your camcorder and VCR.

Exporting to QuickTime

Another option for saving and exporting: You can output your movies to a QuickTime file. When you select the QuickTime option from the pull-down menu in the Export Movie dialog box, iMovie provides a variety of options for compressing your project as a QuickTime movie. Once you have chosen a QuickTime compression format—for email, small Web movies, or CD-ROM—you can let iMovie's sophisticated compression

Exporting Your Movie To save projects to your DV camcorder, choose Export Movie from the File menu.

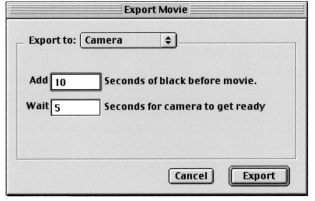

Add a Leader Most camcorders need only a few seconds to prepare for recording, but it's always a good idea to add a few more seconds of black to the tape before the movie is recorded.

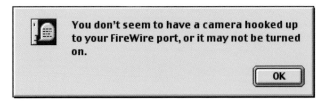

Be Prepared Before you begin exporting, be sure your DV camcorder is connected by the FireWire cable, a videotape is ready to be recorded, and the camera is powered on.

algorithms reduce the large DV file into a compact minimovie that will play in a window on the computer desktop.

Saving Your Movie for CD-ROM

Because of their small size, QuickTime files are an ideal format for inclusion on a CD-ROM. Of course, CD-ROMs are limited to 650MB, which would fill up quickly with large DV files. QuickTime compression creates these files in the best format for getting lots of movies onto a single disc."

As writable DVD drives and media become more accessible and cost-effective, desktop moviemakers may start distributing their movies on DVD.

QUICKTIME PRO

IF YOU INTEND TO DISTRIBUTE YOUR PROJECTS WIDELY, YOU MAY WANT TO LEARN MORE ABOUT QUICKTIME. AN INEXPENSIVE UPGRADE OF THE PRODUCT, CALLED QUICKTIME PRO, PROVIDES EXPANDED EFFECTS AND AUTHORING TOOLS FOR WEB MOVIEMAKERS AS WELL AS EXTENSIVE TRANSLATION CAPABILITIES FOR READING AND CONVERTING OTHER VIDEO FILE FORMATS. FOR MORE DETAILS, VISIT THE APPLE WEB SITE OR GO DIRECTLY TO www.quicktime.com

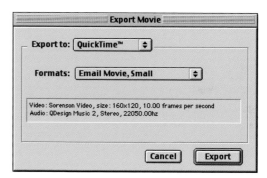

Independence When exporting QuickTime files to your hard drive, iMovie creates an independent movie file that can be transferred to removable media or posted on the Web without referencing the original source footage.

EXPORTING DIRECTLY TO A VCR

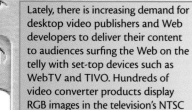

Lately, there is increasing demand for desktop video publishers and Web developers to deliver their content to audiences surfing the Web on the telly with set-top devices such as WebTV and TIVO. Hundreds of video converter products display RGB images in the television's NTSC format, but most manufacturers use a type of "line averaging" to fit your monitor's viewable area into the TV aspect ratio. The result is often a flickering, hard-to-read, box floating inside thick black borders. However, FOCUS Enhancements has introduced its $125 i-TView DV video converter, designed specifically for iMac computers. Its pixel-to-pixel compression technology prevents flicker, enhances small fonts, and fills the entire TV screen with a mirror image of your monitor. For iMac DV users, it's an easier way to record DV movies to a VCR or display them on a TV. You can put your footage straight through the built-in VGA port (a 15-pin mini D-Sub connector hidden behind a flap in the back of your iMac) without putting movies back out to the DV camcorder over FireWire.

Saving Movies for the Web

Web site designers can incorporate their high-quality iMovie movies into the design of their HTML Web pages or offer them on a Web server as downloadable files. In iMovie, the two Web Movie options in the Export Movie dialog box are ideal for compressing your DV footage into reasonable file sizes for distribution over dial-up modems or high-speed Internet connections.

In the next chapter, "Preparing Video for the Web," you'll learn more about other forms of QuickTime compression—specifically, those designed for streaming video over the Internet.

Using the Experts Setting

There is little need to change the compression settings in iMovie; they have been fine-tuned to produce exceptional playback across a variety of systems and speeds. However, at times, more experienced users will wish to tinker with the compression settings. This can be done through the Expert option in the Export Movie dialog box.

"Experts" are those people who need to customize the export settings to instruct the compression software to prepare the final movie files to meet special requirements. For those who prefer to use third-party compression utilities, iMovie will also export movies in a "lossless" compression format, which means the quality of the image will remain at full DV resolution. These lossless files, although technically compressed, retain so much information that the data file is often quite large.

Whether you plan to stream your work on a Web site, share video with coworkers over an office network, or archive a collection of movies on a CD-ROM, you'll need to shrink those stories down to a manageable size first. Saving your movies in a proper format is the key to taking your masterpieces out of the living room and onto the Web.

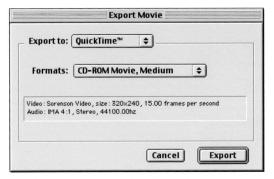

Shrink to Fit Before including video in interactive presentations, you'll need to shrink your movies down to a manageable size by saving them with the CD-ROM settings.

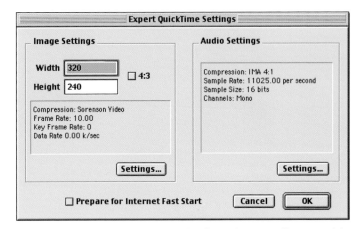

Expert Settings "Experts" can customize the settings according to special requirements. This feature should only be used by those experienced with compression utilites.

preparing video
for the web

The powerful exchange of desktop video over the Internet is akin to the proliferation of ideas in the wake of the printing press, radio broadcasting, desktop publishing, and online communities. The easy analogy is television; a Web site is like a TV station, and every computer become a miniature cable network—offering a unique programming format to the entire world. By using the Internet, movie-makers can instantly share their work

A Web site is like a TV station.

with audiences worldwide instead of being rejected by film festivals and studio executives. iMovie is the first application tailored to creating movies for Web distribution. Powerful compression software is included in the iMovie program to streamline the export of finished footage, preparing it for immediate publishing over the Internet—an aspect of video production that has been gravely overlooked by high-end video packages.

Sending Movies over the Internet

To help you prepare for Internet distribution, iMovie is equipped with special predefined compression settings that will produce excellent Web-ready files in the QuickTime format. By making these QuickTime movies extremely compact, iMac users can easily attach video to email messages or add them to their Web pages so they can share them immediately with friends and family around the world. In fact, many online communities are already sharing their stories over the Web in the QuickTime format.

File Size and Compression

The main objective of video compression software is to shrink the file size of a QuickTime movie down to a bare minimum while salvaging enough data to create rich, fluid movement and fine picture detail. iMovie's export function does this by analyzing each frame of the footage for color, motion, and transitions. Then iMovie disregards redundant information before scaling down each frame and saving it to a new file.

Optimizing video for the Web requires iMovie to squeeze image data to 1/8000 of its original signal quality. This process can be time consuming if you are waiting for iMovie to compress long movies. An Export status bar will appear in the center of your screen, indicating the progress of the compression. Don't worry if the bar doesn't move swiftly; complex footage can take as long as several minutes for each frame. For movies more than a few minutes in length, it's best to leave the computer running and come back after it's finished.

Using the iMovie Web Settings

The "Experts" button should only be used if you have a good understanding of video compression and want to customize the settings for specific project needs. Even then, iMovie's pre-sets will probably produce better results than most so-called experts, as they were specially designed by the developers of today's leading video compression software.

TIP

FILE SIZE RESTRICTIONS
SOME ONLINE SERVICES, WEB SERVERS, OFFICE NETWORKS, AND EMAIL PROGRAMS PUT LIMITS ON THE SIZE OF FILES THEY WILL TRANSFER OVER THE INTERNET. CHECK WITH YOUR SERVICE PROVIDER BEFORE SENDING LARGE MOVIES TO FAMILY AND FRIENDS OVER THE WEB.

Presenting Your Movie on the Web

Movie Players and Plug-Ins

Several of the video and media players available today are completely free to Internet surfers, and some are included in your browser software as multimedia plug-ins. Three of these player technologies have emerged as leaders in the streaming arena.

QuickTime 4

Apple's QuickTime software has been distributed with the Macintosh operating system for years, so iMovie can boast a greater compatibility with this international video player. QuickTime currently has more installed players than others in the field. It's free, and it's already part of most contemporary browsers. It plays nearly any kind of audio or video file and works as an incredibly useful tool—almost as a universal file translator—by supporting more than 200 different formats and

QuickTime The QuickTime player is a utility that plays video files you receive from other people or via the Internet. It comes preinstalled with your iMac DV computer and has similar controls to the Monitor window in iMovie.

instantly converting them to a wide selection of popular media types. The latest release, QuickTime 4, has been optimized for playback of exceptionally high-quality streaming video.

RealPlayer

Much of the Internet's current stockpile of streaming media is available through the RealPlayer technology. What started as an audio-listening plug-in for Web browsers has grown to a multifaceted multimedia application. As a versatile player, it doesn't support a wide variety of formats, but it covers some popular ones such as MP3, JPEG, MPEG, and Flash. Webmasters can also link to a myriad of streaming content provided by Real's portal site. Filmmakers can take advantage of Real's complementary tools and consulting services to help them stream movies to the world. You can download a free player from the Real site at **www.real.com.**

Windows Media Player

Windows Media Player is not as well executed as the Real or QuickTime players. Despite the backing of the world's premier marketing empire, Microsoft NetShow technology and other support modules have a rather unstable reputation. Plus, adoption of the Windows Media Player has been slow. It plays many popular file formats such as AVI and MPEG movies adequately, and handles audio files quite well. But overall, its integration with browsers is shaky and it fails to deliver streaming media reliably. A beta version is also available for the Macintosh at the Windows Media Player Web site, **www.microsoft.com/wmp**.

RealPlayer
RealPlayer streams compressed movies directly over the Internet and presents them in your Web browser for immediate playback. RealPlayer also includes links to streaming sites.

Windows Media Player Microsoft's offers a no-frills alternative for streaming called Windows Media Player. Despite the name, a version is available for the Macintosh as well.

USING EXPERT SETTINGS WITH OTHER COMPRESSION UTILITIES

As the leader of audio and video compression, Media Cleaner Pro 4 includes just about everything video streamers need to master moving pixels. Media Cleaner Pro is a must-have utility for producing lots of compressed video clips. Once installed, you can use Media Cleaner's settings to control the quality of the compressed movie from the "Experts" button inside iMovie's Export dialog box. Its superior algorithms and extensive support of the QuickTime, Real, AVI, and MPEG-1 formats are the reference standard for batch processing. More important, Media Cleaner Pro 4 now exports to the most widely used streaming technologies: QuickTime 4, RealSystem G2, and Windows Media Player. Better yet, Media Cleaner Pro provides a host of preconfigured settings for each player, much like the menu options inside iMovie.

Web Sites Where Movie Watchers Go

Movies are a fast-growing attraction on the Internet. In the past two years, there has been an explosion of sites specializing in short films. Each site has its own conditions and processes for reviewing and showcasing the work. Many post their guidelines online and will even prepare your files for streaming; they will require you to send a Mini-DV tape to them. Most sites accept short films, but some show full-length features. Check the resource files on the DVD-ROM disc for links to these sites, or see the "Related Links" section for a list of URLs.

Posting Movies for Download

Web video has come a long way in a short time. It used to be that there was only one way to share movies over the Internet. Moviemakers would have to compress their video into a single QuickTime file and post it on an FTP server. Then they could encourage people to click a link to access the file for progressive download. Viewers received a copy of the entire file after a long download and were able to play the movie from their hard drive.

When you compress your final movies and make them available from Web pages as progressively downloadable files, you can be sure your video will remain gorgeous no matter where it is seen. Progressive files are slow to compress (and download) but fast and beautiful at playback.

TIP

EMBEDDED MOVIES IN HTML *IF YOU ARE AN EXPERIENCED WEB SITE DESIGNER, YOU MAY WISH TO DISPLAY QUICKTIME MOVIES ON YOUR OWN SITE. THIS CAN BE DONE BY EMBEDDING SOME SIMPLE CODE IN YOUR HTML PAGES. SOME PREFORMATTED HTML TEMPLATES ARE AVAILABLE FOR YOUR FREE USE AT www.makingimovies.com*

Movie Sites Many Web sites now showcase a moviemaker's work, drawing attention to up-and-coming directors. Among the online leaders are ShortBuzz, iFilm, and Atom Films. To link to these sites and others, visit an expanded list of streaming video destinations at **www.makingimovies.com.**

Preparing Video for Streaming

Today, a more common approach for showing video online is streaming technology. Often used for longer files—such as movies—streamed movies differ dramatically from QuickTime files in image quality. Streamed movies are compressed without as many of the details and, subsequently, there are no assurances that your pictures will look good to the viewer. However, streamed movies will arrive in a timely fashion. Video streams are not saved on your hard drive (they are just buffered in 3-second chunks in a small cache file), which means they can't be saved or replayed offline.

With streaming video, the soundtrack is usually delivered without interruption. Whether you choose downloads or streaming for your movies, pay close attention to the audio quality of your movies, and recompress them with different settings if the results are not acceptable.

If you're interested in streaming video from your own desktop or home-made server, Apple's QuickTime and several other applications provide easy ways to send out clips over a local network or the Web. Read the "Related Links" section in the back of the book for a list of some manufacturers' Web sites.

behind the scenes

Making the Tutorial Movies

First Impression

A teenager is asked to hold a skateboard for a friend and, while waiting, is approached by a girl who invites him to the upcoming dance. To impress her, he claims the skateboard as his own and must perform some tricks that are beyond his capabilities. Or are they?

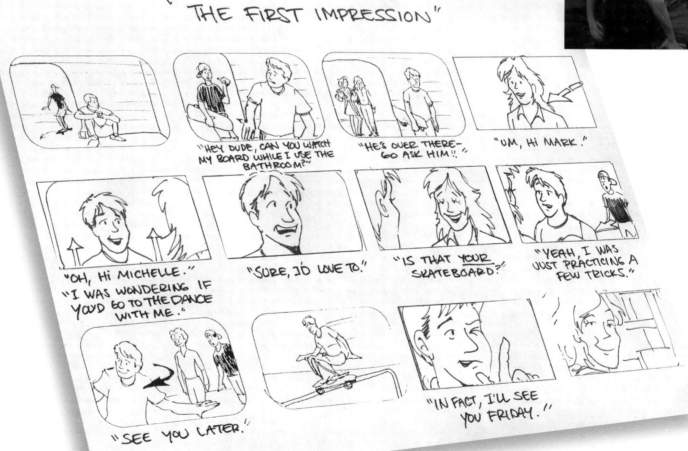

This lesson demonstrates the power of editing. By removing the failed attempts of actor Jason Tsoi to execute the difficult stunts, we combined several clips to give the appearance of a successful first effort. To ensure Jason's safety during these high-flying moments, thick foam padding was placed on the ground to break his fall.

A clear plastic box was placed over the camera in shots where Jason's stunts were headed straight for the lens. As an extra precaution, the camera was left running on a small tripod, without an operator nearby. In most cases, these measures were more than adequate. However, in one instance they saved the camera from certain destruction. Check out the sample movie called "The Wipeout" in the QuickTime Gallery on the DVD-ROM disc.

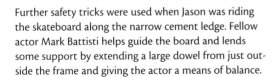

Further safety tricks were used when Jason was riding the skateboard along the narrow cement ledge. Fellow actor Mark Battisti helps guide the board and lends some support by extending a large dowel from just outside the frame and giving the actor a means of balance.

The actors were asked to wear their own clothing and bring their own props (including backpacks and skateboard). Jason wore a simple white shirt because he needed to perform repeated takes over the course of several days; a simple costume was easy to remember. The shooting schedule took advantage of a school break during the holidays; there would be no students to interfere with the actors. However, the high school band class (particularly the drummers) showed up to practice just as shooting began. Their rhythms can be heard throughout several of the takes.

The Flower of Love

A man waits in a hotel room for a rendezvous with a woman he has never met. He reads a letter from his pen pal explaining that she will be wearing a rose on her dress. Suddenly, a woman appears. They embrace, they kiss, they look longingly at each other. When the bellhop arrives and announces the room number, they realize there has been a mistake. The woman abruptly leaves, and the man is momentarily shattered—until the real pen pal shows up.

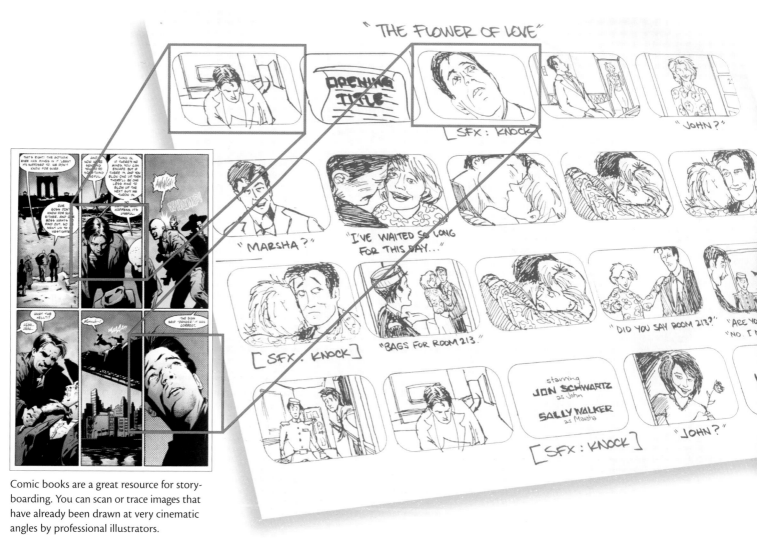

Comic books are a great resource for story-boarding. You can scan or trace images that have already been drawn at very cinematic angles by professional illustrators.

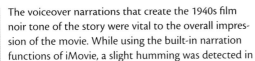

The voiceover narrations that create the 1940s film noir tone of the story were vital to the overall impression of the movie. While using the built-in narration functions of iMovie, a slight humming was detected in the recording, due to the spinning of the hard drive inside the iMac DV computer. To eliminate this buzz, a microphone was placed next to a chair in the hallway, and the actors gave their readings from a distance away. Using external microphones and commercial recording equipment requires a small adapter to import the audio into a Macintosh computer.

Sometimes the most thorough set planning can't foresee simple problems. In the hallway scene, a bright ceiling lamp creates a halo effect above the bellhop's head.

To diminish the glow, some aluminum foil was placed in the glass bowl of the lamp, keeping light from shining on one half of the hallway. The result was a more subdued halo, but the result was still quite distracting.

Instead, the actors were asked to reposition themselves strategically during high points in the action to conceal the lamp from the camera.

Often, great takes are ruined by small oversights. Although two of the actors used in the movie are married in real life, they played characters who are desperately single. Unfortunately, they wore their wedding rings throughout the shoot, which we uncovered only after much of the footage was captured. The two examples shown here were among the best takes available, but they were unusable due to these small but noticeable details. A close examination of the final edit will reveal a glimpse of a wedding ring that unfortunately remains a permanent part of the movie.

This lesson was shot in black and white for a more cinematic feel and a film noir look. But black-and-white photography creates some unique challenges. First, items that are highly reflective will shine unwanted glare into the camera. As a rule, it's best to avoid shimmering jewelry or props that refract light in a distracting way. However, in this particular shot, the action of the man as he tips the bellhop was unclear without the illumination of the metallic surface on the coin. An overhead light was placed behind the camera, aimed at the point of exchange, and the actor was asked to hold the face of the coin at an angle, bouncing the light into the lens. An oversized coin helps to draw attention to the action, as does the silhouette of the actor's arm against the clear background.

General Hysteria

An army general is on the run—alone in the desert wasteland. Throughout his struggles for survival against the unrelenting forces of nature, his memory replays the events that have led him to this desperate fight for life. As the scorching sun sizzles, and vultures swirl above, he suddenly wakes from his nightmare to discover that he is closer to home than first imagined.

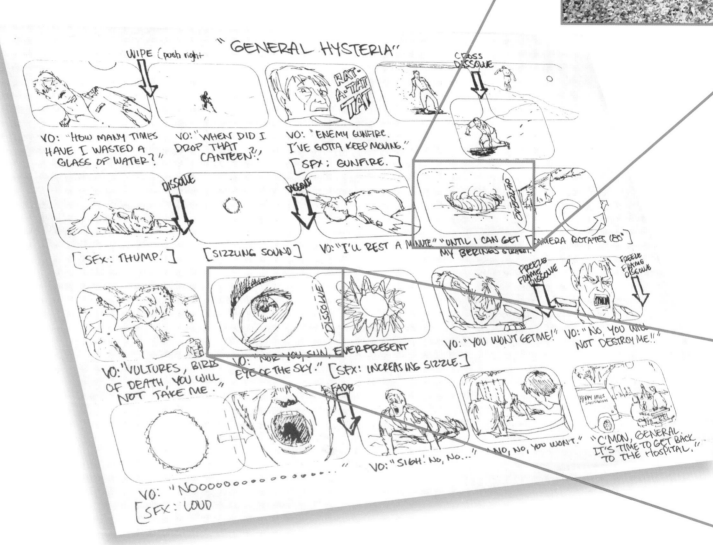

The use of cross-dissolves, fades, and wipes in the movie create a suggestion of the passage of time. The psychological condition of the main character was also reinforced by including footage of a struggling insect—which mirrors the general's battle with the elements.

The narration used in this movie needed to suggest different moments in time, so the actor recorded only part of his dialogue indoors. Other readings were taken outdoors to capture the hollow sound of vast spaces and ambient noises such as wind.

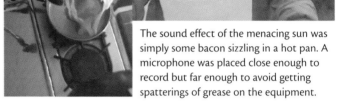

At the beginning of the shoot, the uniform worn by the general was clean and pressed, so it was deliberately soiled on location using mud and sand found around the park. To make the character's shabby appearance even more believable, the lead actor was asked to grow his facial hair for several days.

The sound effect of the menacing sun was simply some bacon sizzling in a hot pan. A microphone was placed close enough to record but far enough to avoid getting spatterings of grease on the equipment.

A tripod can be used for more than stationary shots. To create a sense of unbalance and disorientation in the character's state of mind, a swirling effect was created using an overhead shot and a moving tripod. By extending the legs of the tripod to their maximum length and folding them into a point, you can anchor the tripod and move it as if it were tethered to a single base. The overhead position shown here was equally beneficial to creating an abstract viewpoint for the shot. As the actor sways clockwise, the cameraman moves the tripod in a counterclockwise direction, capturing the unorthodox movement of the final sequence.

No animals were harmed in the making of this movie, but the cast and crew suffered a bit. While enduring the blistering beams of sunlight in his eyes, actor Paddy Morrissey holds still for a slow pan across his face in close-up. Just as he is directed to open his eyes, a small fly lands suddenly on his nose and steps lightly across his face. Although completely unplanned, the happy accident lends a gritty realism to the final movie.

Troubleshooting

The iMovie software is incredibly reliable, but at times you'll need some technical specifications or troubleshooting tips. Apple provides a complete knowledgebase—an online library of detailed product information—which is updated daily and archives more than 14,000 older articles. To search the Apple Technical Information Library, visit its site at **www.apple.com**

System Requirements

The iMac DV models pack extraordinary processing power, exceptional graphics acceleration, and plenty of space for hard disk space of moviemaking. However, if you are attempting to use iMovie on a PowerBook or other Macintosh computer, your system will need to meet these basic requirements:

- A Power Macintosh computer with a PowerPC G3 300 MHz or faster processor

- Mac OS 8.6 or later

- QuickTime 4.0 or later

- 64 megabytes (MB) of random access memory (RAM). iMovie requires a minimum of 16 MB free. On systems with 64 megabytes, be sure Virtual Memory is turned on in the Memory control panel.

- A CD-ROM drive

- 2 gigabytes (GB) of available hard disk space is highly recommended

- A display that supports 800 x 600 resolution and thousands of colors (1024 x 768 in millions recommended)

- A built-in FireWire (IEEE 1394) port

- A 4-pin-to-6-pin FireWire cable (for use with DV camcorder)

- You may need to add a SCSI controller card for external storage drives. And don't skimp on storage. Digitizing video requires transfer speeds of roughly 3.6 MB per second. That means more than 200 MB of disk space may be needed for just one minute of footage. Fortunately, FireWire achieves fast a 400-megabit-per-second transfer rate, making it ideal not only for digital video cameras but for other peripherals such as scanners and mass-storage drives.

Using Other FireWire Capture Cards

Apple's integration of FireWire is by far the most trouble free, offering seamless capture into editing applications and excellent device control of your camcorder. There are several other manufacturers of FireWire add-in cards for capturing footage to older Macintosh computers. Many of these include driver software that conflict with the system extensions installed in your operating system. Check the Apple Web site to make sure you have the most recent version of the FireWire extension (currently, Version 2.2.2). This version adds services to the Mac OS that support the use of different types of FireWire hardware and software.

Running Low on Memory

If you receive an error message that says you are "Running Low on Memory," it is likely that your iMac DV computer is being hindered by other processes. You may need to quit applications other than iMovie that are running simultaneously. On computers with 64 megabytes of RAM, be sure Virtual Memory is turned on in the Memory control panel. You can also increase the amount of RAM allocated to iMovie by following these steps:

1 Quit iMovie.

2 Locate the iMovie application (not the alias) and click once the iMovie application icon to highlight it.

3 Open the File menu and choose Memory from the Get Info submenu.

4 Increase the number in the Preferred Size field to 30720 and then close the window and restart iMovie.

For optimal performance in the application, do not attempt to switch your monitor resolution settings while iMovie is busy rendering title or transition effects.

Tips For Camcorder Compatibility

If you have not yet bought a camcorder, make sure you get a model that specifically says "digital" and comes equipped with FireWire (also called "IEEE 1394" or "i.Link"). The Canon XL1 still reigns among digital FireWire camcorders because it features a lightweight ergonomic design, changeable lenses, and exceptionally strong industry support. But a smaller camcorder, such as Sony's DVCR-PC1 1 CCD MiniDV Camera, may be your best bet. Other smaller models include Canon's Optura and Elura models. Sony's DVMC-DA1 and DVMC-MS1 AV adapters allow the use of non-DV devices such as Hi8 and other analog camcorders. However, these devices do not allow iMovie to control the camcorder. The following DV devices have been qualified for use with iMovie. For the latest information on DV device compatibility, visit the iMovie web site at **www.apple.com/imovie.**

Canon Camcorders

- Elura
- Optura
- Ultura
- Vistura
- ZR

Panasonic Camcorders

- AG-EZ20
- AG-EZ30
- PV-DV710
- PV-DV910

Sharp Camcorders

- VL-PD3

Sony Camcorders

- DCR-PC1
- DCR-PC10
- GV-D300
- DCR-TR7000
- DCR-TRV103
- DCR-TRV110
- DCR-TRV310
- DCR-TRV310E
- DCR-TRV5E
- DCR-TRV510
- DCR-TRV7
- DCR-TRV8
- DCR-TRV9
- DCR-TRV9E
- DCR-TRV900
- DCR-TRV900E

Using Device Control

iMovie includes a feature called device control, which takes over the operations of your digital camcorder once it is connected to the computer by FireWire. If you cannot pause your camcorder during rewind or fast-forward using the on-screen buttons in iMovie, try pressing the Stop button instead of the Pause button before these operations.

Exporting to DV Tape

If you are attempting to export a movie to a DV tape that resides in the camcorder and the LCD flashes the message "Check DV Input," your camcorder may require an updated FireWire driver (version 2.2.2), which can be downloaded for free at `www.apple.com`.

Upon export, some camcorders will immediately enter their REC/Pause mode but never actually start recording. In this case, try the following steps:

1 Stop the camcorder and cancel the export.

2 Add a few extra seconds of black before the recording, or increase the time to wait for the camera in the Export Movie window.

3 When you export to tape, watch for black frames being sent to the camera on the LCD and then press the Still button on the camcorder's VTR controls to begin recording.

4 If this does not work, try pressing the Play button on the camcorder's VTR controls to begin recording.

Storage Device Speed

iMovie needs fast hard disks. When adding more storage devices, you will need disk drives with a sustained transfer rate of 3.6 MB or faster. The following storage devices do not meet the minimum transfer rate or capacity requirements to work with iMovie.

- SuperDisk drives
- Floppy disk drives
- Zip drives
- AppleShare or IP mounted file servers

Reinstalling iMovie

iMovie was installed on your computer in the Applications folder on your hard disk. To reinstall iMovie, open the installer on the iMovie CD and follow the instructions on the screen. The installer will put an iMovie folder containing the iMovie application folder and the iMovie Tutorial folder on the main level of your hard disk. After installation, drag this folder and its contents into the Applications folder to restore it to the original location.

Web References

The following lists feature Web sites of products and companies listed in this book as well as some informative and entertaining destinations for aspiring moviemakers. For a single resource page with all of these hyperlinks, bookmark the Making iMovies site at *www.makingimovies.com*.

Online Showcases and Festivals

Always Independent Films
www.alwaysindependentfilms.com

Atom Films www.atomfilms.com

CinemaNow www.cinemanow.com

D FILM Digital Film Festival www.dfilm.com

Digital Entertainment Network www.den.com

Entertaindom www.entertaindom.com

Eveo www.eveo.com

Icebox Animation www.icebox.com

IFilm Network www.ifilm.net

MediaTrip www.mediatrip.com

The New Venue www.newvenue.com

Pop.com www.pop.com

Reelshort www.reelshort.com

RES Fest www.resfest.com

Short TV www.shorttv.com

SightSound www.sightsound.com

Sputnik 7 www.sputnik7.com

StudioNext www.studionext.com

Trailer Park www.movie-trailers.com

Vidnet www.vidnet.com

WireBreak Shortz www.wirebreak.com

Audio Sites

Sonic Foundry/Sound Forge **www.sonicfoundry.com**

Musicopia **www.musicopia.com**

Sonic Desktop **www.smartsound.com**

Soundtrack Studios **www.soundtrackgroup.com**

The Classical Midi Archives **www.prs.net**

The Music Bakery **www.musicbakery.com**

Public Domain Music **www.pubdomain.com**

Camera Support and Stabilization Systems

Steadicam Jr. and DV Cinema **www.steadicam.com**

Glidecam Industries **www.glidecam.com**

Jimmy Jib **www.jimmyjib.com**

Skateboard Dolly Plans **www.inforamp.net/~bpaton/ skateboard.htm**

Steady Tracker **www.steadytracker.com**

Online Discussion and News Groups

1394 Trade Association **www.firewire.org**

Desktop Video Newsgroup **rec.video.desktop**

Video Production Newsgroup **rec.video.production**

Cineweb's Connections **www.cineweb.com/connections/**

Desktop Video **desktopvideo.miningco.com**

Movie Production **rec.arts.movies.production**

Multimedia Tools **multimediatools.com**

DV Central **www.dvcentral.org**

Global DVC Group **www.global-dvc.org**

Mac Digital Video Resources **www.postforum.pair.com**

DV Cameras and Accessories

Bogen `www.bogenphoto.com`

Canon USA `www.canondv.com`

Hardigg's Cases `www.hardigg.com`

JVC Electronics `www.jvc-america.com`

Markertek Video Supply `www.markertek.com`

NRG Research `www.nrgresearch.com`

Panasonic `www.panasonic.com`

Sony Electronics `www.sel.sony.com`

Sharp `www.sharpusa.com`

Video Smith `www.videosmith.com`

Online Film Schools

Cyber Film School `www.cyberfilmschool.com`

Dov S-S Simens 2 Day Film School `www.hollywoodu.com`

Film.com `www.film.com`

Filmmaker `www.filmmaker.com`

3D Graphics, Animation, Titles, and Special Effects

Adobe Systems `www.adobe.com`

Alien Skin Software `www.alienskin.com`

DigiEffects `www.digieffects.com`

ICE (Intergrated Computing Engines) `www.iced.com`

MetaCreations `www.metacreations.com`

Puffin Designs `www.puffindesigns.com`

Softimage `www.softimage.com`

Strata `www.strata.com`

Moviemaking Magazines and Resources

DV Magazine `www.dv.com`

DVEreview Newsletter `www.dvereview.com`

Filmmaker Magazine `www.filmmag.com`

Interactivity Magazine `www.interactivity.com`

The Internet Movie Database `www.imdb.com`

New Media Magazine `www.newmedia.com`

RES Magazine `www.resmag.com`

Videography Magazine `www.videography.com`

Videomaker Magazine `www.videomaker.com`

The Movie Sound FAQ `www.moviesoundpage.com`

Compression and Streaming Technologies

Akamai **www.akamai.com**

Apple **www.apple.com**

Encoding.com **www.encoding.com**

Microsoft Media Player **www.microsoft.com**

Real Networks **www.realnetworks.com**

Terran **www.terran.com**

FireWire Hardware Manufacturers

Newer Technology **www.newertech.com**

VST Technology **www.vsttech.com**

Medea **www.medeacorp.com**

FirePower **www.firepower.com**

INDEX

A

action shots
    compression and, 18
    setting mood with visual effects, 13
    using silhouettes in, 21
activating
    Audio Timeline, 61, 72, 73
    crop sliders, 46
    Eye-View Timeline, 41
actors, casting, 17
Adding Titles project, 83
Adobe Illustrator file format, 10
Adobe Photoshop
    creating storyboard illustrations in, 11
    importing files from, 10
advertising as story source, 3
AIFF audio files, 75
analog video, 37
angles, composing shots with, 29
animation
    in titles, 81
    Web sites about, 129
Apple PlainTalk microphone, 67
Apple Technical Information Library, 124
Apple Web site, 124
archiving footage on DV videotape, 107
arrow keys
    adjusting master volume level with, 63
    moving playhead or crop sliders with, 42, 45
Atom Films Web site, 115
audio, 60–76
    adding narration to, 67, 68–69
    adding to Audio Timeline, 64–67
    adding to Sounds Effects folder, 76
    avoiding costuming noises, 23
    changing meaning with, 71
    deleting, 65
    duplicating and pasting sound effects, 65

DV format and synchronized, 61
    editing on Audio Timeline, 70–71
    fading, 63
    importance of soundtrack, 60
    importing AIFF audio files, 75–76
    importing music from audio CD, 74–75
    positioning in Audio Timeline, 72–73
    preventing unwanted noise on, 23, 26
    recording ambient noises, 28
    selecting, 61, 63, 72
    setting volume for, 61, 63
    streaming video and soundtrack, 116
    synchronizing with title and transition effects, 103
    turning on/off, 62, 72, 73
    See also narration
audio crop markers, 70
audio resources on Web, 127
Audio Timeline
    activating, 61, 72, 73
    adding audio to, 64–67
    editing audio on, 70–71
    illustrated, 61
    positioning audio on, 72–73
    selecting sound in, 61–63

B

backgrounds
    still images as title, 88–89
    title effects over black, 83–86
    troubleshooting problem, 19–20
batch capturing by timecode, 36
black-and-white movies
    challenges of, 121
    costuming for, 24
    Flower of Love sample movie, xii, 64, 120–121
blurry titles, 88
BMP images, 10
Built-in Mic setting (Sound Monitoring Source pop-up menu), 67

C

camcorders. *See* DV camcorders
camera support and stabilization resources on Web, 128
Capture Mode button, 35
capture sessions
    batch capturing by timecode, 36
    of live video from camera, 37
    running out of disk space, 37
    starting and stopping, 35–36
casting roles, 17
CD-ROM discs
    importing music from audio, 74–75
    saving movies on, 109
CD-ROM drive, 124
checked patterns, 24
choosing title effects, 80
cinematic effects
    avoiding rapidly changing images, 18
    capturing mood and tone, 13
    fading effects, 63, 94
    film noir tone, 121
    importance of soundtrack, 60
    lighting, 27–28
    limiting color choices for iMovies, 81–82
    pros and cons of close-ups, 20
    sound effects and meaning, 71
    sound effects as cues, 66
    staging, 21
    symmetrical shots, 101
    of titles, 79
    See also shooting techniques
Clear command
    deleting clips and sound effects with, 37, 65
    on Edit menu, 56
clearing footage from clip, 56–57
clip art, 8
clip rows, 10
Clip Shelf
    arranging clips on, 8, 10
    dragging clips to timeline from, 42, 48
    importing files to, 12–13
    printing, 13

H

hard drives
    disk space on, 36, 37, 124
    dragging Project File folder to, xiii
    required transfer rate of, 126
hardware
    internal and external microphones, 67
    system requirements for iMovie, 124
    See also FireWire; hard drives
how-to movies, 4–5

I

i.Link. *See* FireWire
icons
    DVD, xi
    eye, 41
    file, 10, 11, 13, 41
    musical note, 61
    sound effects, 61
IEEE 1394. *See* FireWire
iFilm Web site, 115
iMac computer,
    internal and external microphones, 67
    support of FireWire devices, 33–34
    system requirements for iMovie, 124
image quality
    of digital video, 34
    of imported images, 34
    nondestructive preview of images, 79
image size for imported file icons, 11
iMovie software
    about device control, 126
    Audio Timeline interface, 61–63
    camcorder compatibility with, 125
    controlling camcorder from, 35
    Experts Settings for, 110, 113, 114
    fading audio effects, 63
    increasing memory allocation to, 125
    interface for, x, 8
    reinstalling, 126
    system requirements for, 124

technology for title effects, 79
time displays in, 41
transition effects in, 92
troubleshooting, 124–126
See also FireWire; hard drives
Import button, 35
Import File command, 12
Import File dialog box, 12
importing images, 32–38
    changing import preferences, 36
    with FireWire, 33–34
    image quality and, 34
    into iMovie, 35–38
    maximum length of captured footage, 36
    from PICT and JPEG files, 12–13
    previewing footage, 38
    for storyboards, 11
    using graphics as title backgrounds, 88–89
importing music
    from AIFF audio files, 75–76
    from audio CD, 74–75
installing tutorial files, xiii
internal microphones, 67, 121
Internet distribution of Web movies, 113
intimacy and close-ups, 20

J

jitters
    created by backgrounds, 19
    stabilizing camcorder to avoid, 25–26
    zooming and, 20, 22
JPEG images
    importing, 10
    saving from Internet, 11
    as title backgrounds, 89

L

lesson files. *See* tutorial files
lighting, 27–28
    compensating for problem, 121
    outdoor, 27

reflected light from clothing, 24
three-light setups, 28
live video capture sessions, 37
locations, 17
low resolution of preview frames, 38
luminance, 18

M

Making iMovies Web site, 8, 127
making tutorial movies
    First Impression, 118–119
    Flower of Love, 120–121
    General Hysteria, 93, 122–123
master volume level, 63
Media Cleaner Pro 4, 114
memory
    increasing allocation to iMovie, 125
    system requirements for, 124
microphones, 67
Mini-DV tapes, 108, 126
Monitor Preview window, 63
monitor requirements for iMovie, 124
Monitor Window, 8
mood, 13
movie clips
    arranging and selecting icons on Clip Shelf, 10
    batch capturing by timecode, 36
    deleting, 37, 41–42
    dragging multiple, 47
    duplicating, 41
    editing names of icons for, 11
    maximum size for imported, 36
    name length for clip icons, 13
    previewing, 42, 53
    renaming, 37
    restoring, 37, 41, 42, 57
    returning to Clip Shelf, 42
    splitting in two, 51–53
    See also audio

R

RealPlayer, 114
Record Voice button, 68
recording
    ambient noises, 28
    audio on DV camcorders, 26
    Flower of Love narration, 121
    music onto audio clip, 75
    narration, 67, 68–69
    rate per second of digital video, 41
red status bar, 84
reinstalling iMovie, 126
remote servers, capturing video to, 37
removing tutorial files, xiii
renaming movie clips, 37
rendering
    multiple transitions simultaneously, 97
    stopping, 85, 86
    of title effects, 84, 86
Resources folder, 76
restoring
    audio clips, 65
    movie clips, 37, 41, 42, 57
    tutorial files, xiii

S

sample movies. *See* DVD-ROM disc
Save Project command, 107
saving, 106–110
    adjusting compression settings before, 110
    cropped footage, 57
    and exporting, 107–109
    to Mini-DV tapes, 108
    movies for Web, 110
    movies on CD-ROM, 109
    project files, 107
    QuickTime movies in DV Stream format, 36
    undoing vs., 57, 71
scripts, 6

selecting
    costuming, 24
    DV camcorders, 25
    multiple audio clips by volume, 61
    prerecorded sound effects, 63
    sound in Audio Timeline, 61–63
shooting techniques, 14–29
    avoiding 16:9 format, 26
    camera movement, 23
    close-ups, 20
    compensating for compression, 18
    composition, 28–29
    contrast vs. color, 19
    costuming, 23–24
    for DV camcorders, 25–26
    for Flower of Love, 121
    lighting, 27–28
    long shots and silhouettes, 21
    moving within single setup, 22
    neighborhood locations, 17
    recording ambient noises, 28
    shooting without scripts, 6
    staging, 22
    Web as movie media, 18
ShortBuzz Web site, 115
silence on set, 26
Silent Flower.mov sample movie, 83
silhouettes
    clear staging and, 21
    dramatic effect of, 28
SimpleText, 13
16:9 format, 26
Sony Digital8 Handycams, 34
Sony DVMC-DA1 Media Converter, 37
sound, 59–76
    adding narration to, 67, 68–69
    adding to Audio Timeline, 64–67
    avoiding costuming noises, 23
    changing meaning with sound effects, 71
    copying to Sounds Effects folder, 76
    deleting, 65

    duplicating and pasting sound effects, 65
    DV format and synchronized audio, 61
    editing audio clips on Audio Timeline, 70–71
    fading audio, 63
    importance of soundtrack, 60
    importing AIFF audio files, 75–76
    importing music from audio CD, 74–75
    positioning audio clips in Audio timeline, 72–73
    preventing unwanted noise on, 26
    recording ambient noises, 28
    selecting prerecorded sound effects, 63
    setting volume for, 61, 63
    streaming video and, 116
    synchronizing with title and transition effects, 103
    turning on/off audio tracks, 62, 72, 73
sound effects icon, 61
Sound Monitoring Source menu, 67
Sounds palette, 63, 72
space bar, starting and stopping imported footage with, 34
special effects
    selecting from Sounds palette, 63, 72
    Web sites for, 129
    See also title effects; transition effects
splitting clips, 51–53
stabilizing camcorders, 25–26
staging, 21–22
starting
    capture sessions, 35–36
    import of DV footage, 34
    movie story, 6–7
stopping
    capture sessions, 35–36
    import of DV footage, 34
    rendering, 85, 86
storage devices, 126
    See also hard drives

V

VHS format, 108

video
about digital, 34
capturing live, 37
converting analog to digital, 37
recording rate per second for digital, 41
streaming, 116, 129
See also DV camcorders; streaming video

video clips
arranging on Clip Shelf, 8
on Audio Timeline, 61
superimposing titles over, 86

video track
appearance of on Audio Timeline, 61
behind title effects, 86–87
See also audio; movie clips

videotape care, 107

View Mode button, 35

viewing
imported footage, 38
with movie players and plug-ins, 113–114
title effects with finished movie, 91
See also playback performance; previewing

voiceover narration. *See* narration

volume
adjusting master volume level, 63
fading audio, 63
selecting multiple clips by, 61
setting for clips, 62–63

W

Warp Out transition effect, 102

Wash In/Wash Out transition effect, 101

WAV files, 76

Web movies, 112–116
choosing title effects for, 81
embedding movies in HTML, 115
Experts Settings for compression, 110, 113
Internet distribution of, 113
overview, 112
posting for download, 115
preparing for streaming video, 116
on QuickTime Player, 113–114
on RealPlayer, 114
saving, 110
Web sites showing, 115
on Windows Media Player, 114

Web sites
Apple, 124
audio, 127
for camera support and stabilization systems, 128
for compression and streaming technologies, 129
for DV cameras and accessories, 128
for FireWire hardware manufacturers, 129
Making iMovies, 8, 127
for moviemaking magazines and resources, 129
online discussion and news groups, 128
for online film schools, 128
showing Web movies, 115
for 3D graphics, animation, titles, and special effects, 129

white balance settings, 27

Windows Media Player, 114

Wipeout sample movie, 119

Z

zooming, 20, 22, 23

Colophon

This book was created with QuarkXPress 4.1, Photoshop 5.0.2, and Illustrator 8.0.1 on a Macintosh G3. The fonts used were Kepler, Cronos, and European Pi from Adobe Inc. and Letter Gothic 12 Pitch from Bitstream Inc. Final output was on a CREO Prinergy Work Flow CTP and it was printed on 80# Orion Matte at Commercial Documentation Services in Medford, OR.

DATE DUE			